John Sellens – an electronics and mechanical engineer,
international businessman and an avid fisherman!

John's career at Thorn EMI Electronics started in design and
trials with UK Military and Defence at home and to over 100
territories globally. He became manager of International Sales
and Marketing Asia and Pacific region, later managing Thorn
Electronics' Corporate activities in Riyadh, residing in Saudi
Arabia for several years. After senior positions in the defence
industry, John's career moved into Fire and Security Systems
becoming managing director of UTC Fire Safety Middle East
based in Dubai, responsible for group business in the Middle
East, Central Europe, North Africa, Central Asia, Russia and
the CIS. He led a successful and motivated international team
– some dedicated fishermen amongst them.

For their continued help, support and encouragement, my grateful thanks to both, professor Larry Hollingworth CBE, and Linda A Ewington.

John Sellens

REELS AND DEALS –
ANGLING FOR BUSINESS

AUSTIN MACAULEY PUBLISHERS™

LONDON • CAMBRIDGE • NEW YORK • SHARJAH

A CIP catalogue record for this title is available from the British Library.

ISBN 9781398433540 (Paperback)
ISBN 9781398433557 (Hardback)
ISBN 9781398433571 (ePub e-book)
ISBN 9781398433564 (Audiobook)

www.austinmacauley.com

First Published 2023
Austin Macauley Publishers Ltd®
1 Canada Square
Canary Wharf
London
E14 5AA

To my wife, my three daughters and their families. To my sister, and with special thanks to our mum and dad, as without them, it would never have happened. To all of the friends and colleagues and those who have been present in my lifetime journey, this book is for you.

Table of Contents

Foreword

I have known John Sellens for thirty years. We share a number of interests. We are collectors of a variety of ephemera. He has travelled further, met more people and amassed much more than I. John, by nature, is relaxed, easy going and good fun to be with socially. Professionally, he is driven, dynamic, determined and very successful.

Earlier this year, we travelled together to a private gathering of collectors of China. We swapped stories and John said, "I really should write down where I have been and what I have done, just for the sake of my children and grandchildren." I threw out a challenge, "Don't talk about it. Do it."

Three weeks later, John sent me the first draft chapters written on his Blackberry phone – driven and determined! It was written from memory, no notes, no consultations, no cross references. Finally, twenty-two chapters.

What amazes me is his total recall: names, dates, events, conversations, cameos. Sitting with him and going through the draft of the book, he adds extra anecdotes, details of the places, the weather, the moods and the context.

A theme throughout the book is that John shapes his own career and also benefits from a large slice of luck. From his earliest days at EMI to his closing days in Dubai and the many places in between, as one door closed, another opened, and John changed companies and climbed another rung of the ladder.

The book isn't all work, his number one hobby, which he shared so much with his father, is fishing, and there are plenty of fisherman's tales to hook us in, from a boy off Southend Pier, catching dabs and whiting, to hauling in a huge stingray from the sea in the UAE, when his father was well into his eighties.

So, in the space of a month, John has ticked off one of his 'bucket list' items. He has a book to give to each of the members of his tribe: to wife Annette, to the three girls, to the thirteen grandchildren and to the twelve great grandchildren.

Now is the time for John to open up the Blackberry once again to write a text book or two to support the academic lectures which he has been invited to give to business schools.

Professor Larry Hollingworth, CBE.

Chapter 1
The Beginning

I was born on September 1st in Walthamstow E17, the first and only son to my father, Frank Hammond Sellens, and my mother, Irene. My sister, Mary Eleanor, was born some two years later at the Perivale maternity hospital, known then as 'the sausage factory'!

We came from an ordinary background; my mum's dad (William Pearson), was a cabinet maker and her mum (Nell Adams), a French polisher. My dad's father, (William), was a postman who was awarded a medal for delivering the mail throughout the war years in London. My grandmother, (Kate), was an eccentric and highly talented concert pianist who played before the King and Queen before her teens. She had her own band and played the music off side stage to accompany the silent movies.

Dad was stationed in Rhodesia (now Zimbabwe), with the RAF doing pilot training during much of the war, returning to England in late 1944. After being demobbed, he joined the Southern Electricity Board as a salesman, where he stayed until retirement at age 65. Mum was a shorthand typist who worked throughout the war in London for Warner Brothers (the film makers) and doing ARP duty at night. My mother and father both passed away in their nineties, having had a long and happy life together.

Schooling for me started at Greenford Infants School at the age of five (this was starting age then), although I ran away on day two, having decided "this is not for me!" We lived two doors away from that school but next, I went to Costains Junior School, all boys at the time, which was a ten-minute walk from home. From memory it was uneventful, always around bottom of the class in each year and failing my 11-plus. Later, I went to Horsenden Secondary Modern School, again a boy's school of the time and this was a short bus ride from home or a forty-minute walk to save the fare, always worthwhile! Here again I hung around bottom of most classes of forty-three pupils but I excelled in woodwork and in metal work. My reading, either interest in, or capacity for, was not up to much and at fifteen, I struggled to read as Mum would point out, often stating that I would never achieve much in life! My sister was the apple of my mum's eye and 'the clever one'. She did go to London University, studying theology, but then married a vicar; she completed teachers' training and finished a degree through Open University later in life.

I spent much of my time with Grandad Pearson in my first ten years and during school holidays learning wood working and general DIY skills from him – very happy days.

My DIY activities paid dividends as during the school holidays, when I was fourteen; I erected a new garden fence for the old chap next door. He gave me a one-pound Premium Bond (they were a very new scheme) which won the top prize of 1000 pounds in its first draw. A huge amount of money in those days and it was shared and spent wisely.

My real interest from the age of about four, was coarse fishing with my dad and this stayed with me through most of my life even after Dad passed away, although latterly it became sea, rather than river fishing, but I will deal with this later in the book. My dad was an excellent fisherman, having been a member of the famous Warwick Angling Society in Walthamstow in his early days. His father, and a number of the Pearson tribe, were also members. Most of my early years were spent fishing in the wonderful river Thames, always with my dad, and I became very good. We joined the Hoover Company Fishing Club based in Perivale when I was ten and soon started to win many junior competitions, so much so that I had to fish against the seniors from the age of thirteen! My dad and I won the majority of the competitions for about seven more years, primarily on the Thames, on London Angler's Association Waters and the Hampshire Avon. The Hampshire Avon was fished in competitions once a year and Dad and I won every time, we really were that good as my trophy cabinet proves. My mother seemed to think I could only succeed at fishing but Dad and I were inseparable with a rod in our hand and this was the diamond in my upbringing. In my early teens I started, with Dad's encouragement, to get involved and interested in repairing radios and televisions and all things electrical, little did I know this would start my career in electronics.

I left school at fifteen with three O levels: Metalwork, Geography and Maths and at this time, was nearly top of the fifth form so it can be seen that academic achievement at my school was very poor. Just before my sixteenth birthday, I purchased my first car which was a knackered Ford Popular, sit up and beg which cost twenty-five pounds. It was a wreck on four wheels but just what I thought I needed to learn to drive and all I could afford at the time. I worked hard to make it roadworthy and started to learn about cars and how they work, or why they don't. Now I needed someone to teach me to drive and Mr Wright, who lived next door, offered. He was a retired army sergeant major, a very kind man and friend of the family. He said to put in for the test immediately as the waiting list was long – the test date came through by return for two weeks' time! Mr Wright said, "No problem!" and I had two lessons, one a hundred-mile drive to the coast and back, which was very stressful, and second around the test area for an hour. He said, "Perfect, take the test, you are fine!" This I did, and amazingly passed, even in a clapped-out old Ford, my very lucky day. The examiner told me he had felt safe but I needed more practice! I managed to keep the old banger going for over a year and then went upmarket with an old Austin A40 (registration 123 UMH), bought for 140 pounds, and which lasted for a number of years.

Dad encouraged me to try for an electronics apprenticeship as this was 'the coming thing'. I wrote, with help, to EK Cole, the radio and TV manufacturer and EMI at Hayes, who both offered me an interview and afterwards a job – amazing! I took the EMI offer as the journey to work was easier and at three pounds, fifteen pence a week, I started on September 4th 1961, just three days after my sixteenth birthday.

Father And Son Set New Trophy Record
Hoover Angling Society

Perivale angling section results

FATHER AND SON SET
NEW TROPHY RECORD

THE FATHER and son combination of Frank and John Sellens set up a new scoring record in the Perivale angling section's Bell Trophy competition. John Sellens won with 108¾ points, with his father finishing runner-up, 3½ points behind.

The Bell Trophy points system is based on match results and the weight of fish landed and this season is the first that anyone has topped 100 points.

The angling society's big fish specialist is Frank Staniland, who works on inspection in the Perivale paint shop. He set up a new club record by winning four specimen fish cups.

Frank weighed in the biggest bream, chub and perch of the season. His 8lb.10oz. 8dr. chub was equivalent to 38.8 per cent of the British chub record and won him the specimen fish shield.

The angling society's annual meeting is to be held in the Perivale lecture room at 5.15 p.m. on Monday, April 6.

The date for the annual dance is Saturday, April 25, at the Sports Pavilion, North Wembley.

One of the chief guests is expected to be the society president Frank Treggiden, second floor superintendent. Mr.

Treggiden took over the presidency from W.C. Bell, former Hoover Limited director.

TROPHY RESULTS

Roach cup: S. Monle (1lb. 3ozs.)

Bream cup: R. Staniland (3-14-8)

Chub cup: R. Staniland (3-10-8)

Perch cup: R. Staniland (1-3-8)

Best specimen R. Staniland (34.8 per cent of record)

Dace cup: J. Sellens and H. Russell (7ozs)

Four-man team winners: J. Sellens, T. Russell, T. Dunkley, A. Cummings.

Knock-out cup: J. Sellens. Runner-up: H. Russell

Junior Trophy: T. Dunkley. Runner-up: C. Woods.

(Fishing Club, 1965)

Dad and myself at the awards. We won!

Dad at Oxford (1964)

Chapter 2
Learning to Work and Study

My five-year EMI craft apprenticeship started on September 4th, 1961 and was my first experience of real work, although I had worked every Saturday in a hardware shop in Greenford, called 'Lanes', owned by Charlie Brackley for at least five years previously.

The journey from 238, Oldfield Lane, Greenford to EMI at Hayes, Middlesex was a long bus journey on the number 105 with a walk at both ends. The bus went through Southall and we always joked that you needed a visa to pass through as even then, it was known as 'little India', and overall took about an hour to get to work. It was a hell of a walk which I did a number of times in thick fog or heavy snow when the buses stopped running. The clock-in at the factory was at 7.30 am with a three-minute grace period or you lost money and clock-out at 5.30 pm or perhaps later with some overtime, lunch was for one hour with clocking in and out for full worker control. The aim was to get 'staff status', which meant an 0830 start, sign-in, not clock-in, and the use of the staff toilets and staff canteen, oh joy, but seems archaic in this day and age where things are so liberal. My first brief uplift to 'staff status' was during my time in the Training School which

I will come to later. In the factory, we had music in the morning during workers' playtime on the BBC Light Programme, which often had workers breaking into song, the Sid Philips Band was always popular, I seem to remember. The speaker system was also used to indicate lunch break and home time. These really were happy times and what a learning time in industry, the weekly pay packet was very acceptable and a great moment each Friday afternoon was a brown envelope with perforated holes so you could count the contents before opening! It was a godsend though when I learned to drive, had the car, my Ford Popular was luxury and comfort with no frills, no heater fitted and certainly no radio.

An EMI apprentice would normally start in the company Training School first, four months if you were in electronics or one year if you were mechanical. However, the School was full so I went straight into the factory inspection department (now called Quality Assurance). Coil winding, run by Jack Richards, what an eye opener with about fifty staff, two thirds of which were middle aged women! My secondment was four months learning a lot – the language from the ladies was obscene for a shy young lad like me!

In parallel, I started to study for my Ordinary National Certificate (S1) at Southall Technical College, which, even in 1961, was predominately Indian. I enjoyed those four months and afterwards expected a good move to a great department, it was in fact 'Goods Inwards' – oh joy, this was the pits and I nearly quit. You got a copy of the component order from the office, a copy of the drawing and specification from the drawing office. Then collected the item or items from the stores, unpacked them all and inspected them. If they were correct, you stamped the release document with your issued stamp (mine was number 82) and moved the goods back to the stores to be issued to the relevant department. This was a necessary job but very boring. After much complaining to Mr. Gilbert the Manager and four months, they moved me into the Training School.

Some background on EMI: the company was founded in 1887 as The Gramophone Company and is still sometimes referred to as The Gram. HMV (His Masters Voice with the dog and trumpet logo) was launched in March 1931 and is still used today. The Group was a major British conglomerate called EMI which initially stood for Electrical Musical Industries but this was dropped to just EMI in the 70s, publicly, the group was globally known as the number one record and tape supplier, however there was so much more in the electronic field including radios, television, TV cameras, tape recorders, computers, the brain scanner and medical products and a very expansive range of military high-tech products and systems. Most of the electronic products were designed and patented by EMI engineers and significantly contributed to World-War-2 efforts with many radar systems provided. During subsequent years, many of these defence type products were supplied to the army, air force and navy, not only for UK MOD but, with the required approvals, sold for export which was to be a major influence in my life as I will describe later.

I started in the Training School, which was a basic machine shop with lathes, milling machines, drills saws and etcetera, plus about 25 student benches. The man in charge was Mr Silk (ex-Sergeant Major retired) and two instructors. The initial meeting with Silk did not go well, he said, "Sellens, you are here for a year!"

I said, "No, Mr Silk, I am electronics which means four months." His angry response was to inform me that I would not leave until I had made all the test pieces to drawing and he had passed them and this would take twelve months, no ifs or buts. This man was a real tyrant and I believed he was on a mission to break students and fail them or make them quit. He tried every which way to cause me to fail but I completed the full course with all test pieces completed and passed. I left in exactly four months with top marks. I moved on to a new inspection role working on Bloodhound and Thunderbird guided weapon control units. This secondment went well, lasting for about six months. I then was moved to testing Seacat guided weapon control units in a clean room which housed about fifteen workers. I had a great boss, George Davies, who got me playing golf every Saturday. This was a happy time and the secondment lasted a year. I was then interviewed and offered a major advancement into another specialised clean room with two air locks to get in (for the day) to work on a new missile system called Seaslug 2. The boss was Freddy Byron, a very well dressed, smart man who I liked and respected but who was difficult to talk to. The clean room was clinical, housing about twelve people, like a prison but I liked it, learned a lot and worked there for a year before being offered a great promotion for an apprentice, to work in the Defence Technical Section for Pip Piper, an excellent engineer, easy to talk to and a fine boss. This was a small team of whiz kids, eight very clever engineers who dealt with any and all production issues related to quality and operational performance, this was my lucky day it also enabled me to meet everyone on every project in every department throughout all the defence sites and to have a special security pass for complete access. A privileged job, wonderful to learn and meet people and allowing me to continue my Ordinary National Certificate studies on day release plus one evening a week none of which was going that well (fishing was still a big priority). This aspect of work lasted until after my five-year apprenticeship was completed.

During the latter part of my five-year apprenticeship, I took a bar job in Eton, near the bridge over the Thames, a place called 'Skinners', a 'members only' drinking club owned and run by Brian Bleach and his wife. It was an old club rumoured to have been owned by Diana Dors when she was married to Hamilton in the 1950s, also rumoured that orgies were regular occurrences in the 50s with two-way mirrors in the bedrooms! I worked three nights a week, Tuesdays 2000hrs until midnight, Fridays 2000hrs until 0400hrs and Saturdays with similar hours, also every Christmas Eve, New Year's Eve and all bank holidays, the pay was good but I was continually tired during the two years I worked there. It was interesting to meet the clientele, some of which were upper class, others who just thought they were! It was good training to mix with all types and learn about people – you can learn a lot behind the bar, some customers can treat you like dirt, like a servant, the whole experience helped me so much later in life in understanding people and above all to have patience.

Chapter 3
My First Big Break

Having married Annette Bernice Holland towards the end of my apprenticeship, I was still living with Mum and Dad, who had moved from Greenford to Bourne End, Buckinghamshire. My travel to EMI was in the Austin A40, my second car; the first, the knackered old 'sit up and beg' Ford Popular having given up a while back after a good run!

Money was very short, although I was now on 1000 pounds a year, which I had been led to believe was the target to show you had made it – I don't know where that came from! I therefore went into a car sharing syndicate with Sid Wright, Ron Waxman and Dick Marley, the latter had a company car and we all worked at EMI at Hayes and lived in Bourne End. They worked in Ground Radar, Radar Drawing Office and Tape Factory respectively. After a while Dick was replaced by Ted Stratford who worked on tape recorder production.

The journey to work took about thirty minutes if our cars kept going, as apart from Dick's, all were worn out. On one of these journeys, Sid said that there was a vacancy where he worked in Ground Radar PDS (Post Design Services) for an intermediate radar engineer which might interest me. I said that I was only a junior engineer so did not meet the criteria.

Sid said to apply anyway and if I was interested, he would arrange an initial meeting with the manager Bert Budd, which he subsequently did.

A very nervous John went to meet Mr Budd, a really nice guy and good engineer, who I thought was a god, he said I was a bit too junior but to apply anyway via personnel (now Human Resources). I duly applied and, as expected, was rejected by them as too junior. About four weeks later, I met Mr Budd by chance on the street and he said, "I am disappointed in you, I told you to apply for my vacancy and you did not bother." I said that I had applied formally and was rejected by personnel, his response was to tell me to go straight back to my office and wait for a telephone call!

The call came through within an hour from personnel, who claimed there had been a mix up in my application with a post in Airborne Radar; would I attend an interview with Mr Budd in Ground Radar immediately? I went along. The interview was quick, with him saying just that he didn't like being conned; did I want the job? Of course, my answer was yes and I was transferred within a few weeks! The moral of the story here is to never take no for an answer, or give up.

Ground Radar was a fantastic place with dozens of incredibly clever engineers working on many very secret projects. My first reaction was to think I have made it and this would be the pinnacle of my working success, but I was wrong.

PDS was totally working with in-service MOD equipment and Bert had a team of about eight highly experienced engineers, plus me. I felt out of my depth, but the whole team was always helpful, offering assistance when needed. The thing that Bert really taught me was team building and report writing which helped me so much in later years.

The equipment I worked on was called Green Archer, primarily a mortar locating radar, X-band (a frequency of 9.6GHz) and mounted on a four-wheel chassis, with a one-ton diesel silent generator towed behind, by today's standards massive but that was almost state of the art at the time. This equipment was also exported to a number of friendly countries.

This project exposed me to my first overseas visit for the company, to change the aerial system on a number of systems exported to Germany but mounted on tracked vehicles. The visits entailed going by lorry with the equipment to the German Artillery School at Idar Oberstein. Three visits were needed and I went twice, once with Sid Wright and once with Ron Williamson, both of these men became long-term, genuine friends.

Another good spin off was that I was currently studying A1 for my Higher National Certificate and the overseas visit interfered with this and Bert agreed I could repeat the year, my saviour, as I would have failed first time around.

Germany was a great experience and perhaps was the start of me getting the travel bug. The activities in PDS were an excellent learning curve and with a lot of help from Ron Williamson I managed to pass A1 with some endorsements and moved on to A2 which actually seemed to be getting easier! Perhaps my studying brain had at long last got into gear.

I was then loaned onto a new project, called Cymbeline, which I will describe later, in a minor design role. Little did I know, this move would change my life forever as I began to realise that electronic design was not for me. I was not clever enough and did not like dealing with parts of a major system. I wanted to deal with the complete system. I also became aware that I could get on with people at different levels; this became a key factor in my progression in business. I soldiered on in design, learning all the time until my second big break emerged from the mist.

I did another visit to Germany with two EMI personnel, a tank driver and a production engineer. We were to make modifications on tracked vehicle installations on US made M113, armoured personnel carriers, fitted with EMI radars, the location was a German tank factory near Köln. All great, but on the outward journey, our production engineer, Ginger Evans, a great and funny guy, informed me that he hated the Germans, having spent four years in a prisoner of war camp in Poland and having done the famous long winter march across Europe, during which two thirds of the prisoners died! He said he would kill any German he did not like or who approached him and also any guard dog seen, with immediate effect. A plus point was that, unbeknown to anyone, he spoke fluent German, which was not surprising considering his over four years of internment. What a good start to a two-month visit by a young engineer, me! However, we did the jobs without incident but it was a worrying time, another good learning experience on how to handle people (and myself!) in extreme situations.

Chapter 4
Cymbeline

The equipment was an X-Band (frequency of 9.6 GHz) radar with the prime role of locating mortars and in a secondary role, controlling helicopters, locating rockets, directing artillery, ground surveillance, plus quick survey and coastal surveillance. The equipment was developed under a joint venture with the MOD as a lightweight equipment based on a two-wheeled trailer, pulled by a Land Rover which could be deployed on the trailer or lifted off by four men for independent deployment. Some customers required the radar to be mounted onto an armoured tracked vehicle or a mix of the two variants which could be done. It was my belief, however, that mounting on a two-wheeled trailer, towed by a Land Rover, gave maximum flexibility as required in the original design parameters. The equipment was state of the art and, at that time, unique.

The mortar is a devastating weapon even in this world of high-tech military products and has been key in infantry warfare for decades. The standard calibre in the British Army and NATO is now 81 mm, but some armies use the 120 mm (like the Germans). In the last war, two and three inches were used, the former in close quarter battle. The weapon can be deployed within minutes and a number of rounds fired very quickly with point detonation, delayed detonation or air burst by dropping the bomb down a tube fixed to a base plate to initiate firing. The Russians were clever and their standard calibre is 82 mm, so they have the option to fire captured ammunition (less accurate but practical). I saw the world's largest mortar in Finland with a calibre of 300 mm, which was breach loaded. The standard mortar has a maximum range of about eight km and an average time of flight of much more than thirty seconds and has a fixed trajectory (parabola). The latter is key for mortar locating radars. In simple terms, the Cymbeline mortar locating radar, like its predecessor, Green Archer, puts a radar beam into the sky (like a torch beam of approximately two degrees square) scanning an arc of approximately forty degrees, the bomb is recorded as it passes through the beam, this beam is then elevated and the same bomb recorded again as it passes through the beam, the time between the two points is measured. Knowing this and other data, and the position of the radar, (already surveyed in by the gunners) the launch point or impact point is calculated by the internal computer, and a grid reference displayed. This process, in less time than the actual time of flight of the mortar bomb, is passed to the artillery, where retaliatory fire can be initiated. It is interesting that the radar beam sees the tail fin of the mortar bomb, not the main body of the bomb! Electronically and mechanically, very specialised equipment, and at the time, due to its size and weight, the EMI radar was unique with huge export potential as well as supporting our locating operators in our own military.

I started to work to understand the deployment and operation of the system as well as the overall and individual workings of the electrical and mechanical elements. It seemed to me that with a group of individual experts, not many understood the overall operational use and how to deploy it. The exception was Major Geoffrey Corris, an ex-gunner and academic, a world expert on locating mortars who effectively ran the project in the end as well as export sales. A great man in my book with many enemies in the company but had my total respect from day-one and we became close friends over the years and he treated me professionally at all times and latterly like a son.

Although I did not realise it at the time, I was grooming myself to be a field engineer, to deal with the customer, (initially for UK MOD) with the complete Cymbeline radar system and to understudy Peter Mizen, the only trials/field man at the time. Peter was a good man, but had a number of weaknesses and was perhaps a bit of a prima donna, thinking himself indispensable, which none of us is, of course, such a belief in extreme situations can help get the job done!

I was asked to support Peter on Cymbeline trials for a few weeks at the UK Artillery School at Larkhill, near Salisbury, a great opportunity and my first exposure to the British serving army. Things went well and I got on well with the trials officer Major Tony Rioch and his team and started to learn about the UK military, its' structure and way of doing things. I was also introduced to Andy Anderson, a retired major in the gunners who had joined Corris at EMI, we became very good friends and travelled the world together in the coming years; as nice, as kind a man as you could ever meet and he taught me so much. Another mentor figure to whom I owe so much for my military education plus much else besides.

On my one and only visit to Israel, accompanied by Andy Anderson, we had some strange experiences. I was there to review some equipment warranty claims but took the opportunity to do some sight-seeing on our only day off, this was interesting but everything was highly-commercialized. On our return to the hotel, hot and tired, we went to the bar which was empty except for two ladies. We ordered our beer and one of the ladies said to Andy, "Would you like to buy us a drink?" He replied, "Why not? But what you're selling, we are not buying." Good old Andy, and after much discussion, they bought us beers and the ground rules were established. Over the coming days, we got to know this couple of ladies quite well, once they knew we did not want their 'wares' they were really interesting to talk to and even took us out for dinner one evening and paid the bill. They even recommended a good local restaurant called Mandy's Place, which was owned and run by Mandy Rice-Davies of Christine Keeler and Profumo scandal fame of the early 60s! She seemed a nice woman and waited on us and sat with us, talking on a number of occasions, you can only speak as you find. I did not particularly like Israel; the local people I met seemed arrogant and not friendly. Fortunately I never visited again for various reasons.

We had a firing demonstration set up on the Larkhill ranges for a team from South Africa who could be the first export customer if all went well. Now the problem; Mizen was going on a planned overseas holiday which he refused to change. What an opportunity for me to shine! Tony Rioch said he was happy with me and Major Ray Shortland, his replacement, also supported my ability. Corris was concerned and recommended a couple of alternatives from EMI unknown to the Larkhill trials team, so I got the job, what a break!

The South African team were all experts, some from ARMSCOR, and it's true to say Cymbeline at this stage was very unreliable and poor in performance, but the sales visit had to go ahead. All went well at first, then, the main electronic unit (the heart of the system) failed. I thought we were done and Corris was apologising and saying, "Let's go to lunch."

When the leader of the team turned to me and said, "What would you do in a battle situation?"

I said, "Fix it."

He conferred with Corris, then said, "Delay lunch, we'll watch Sellens fix the problem!" Holy of holies, what a challenge but, after about two hours, everything was back together and working. I had saved the day and an order was subsequently placed. I was the talk of the town, Mizen was put out to grass and I was appointed the number one field engineer.

The performance and reliability of the system was so poor, a halt in production was decided for redesign purposes. Corris took overall charge and my few weeks at Larkhill turned into four years living in the 'Rose and Crown' near Bulford Camp. This proved lucrative in expenses and provided wonderful entertainment in Southampton and Bournemouth on a regular basis. Me, a young field engineer, now turned into an artillery expert and an even better expert on Cymbeline – after redesign and many trials on Salisbury Plain, the equipment was a world beater.

An initial order for four Cymbeline systems was received and these were supplied to Oman, possibly as a gift from UK

MOD; I am not sure of this but the systems would be actively used in the war with South Yemen.

It was about this time that I was called by the MOD to a meeting in Admiralty Arch with the Security Services and signed an extract of the official secrets act, enough said.

I received a phone call one Sunday morning from Corris who said, "Will you go to Oman to deliver four Cymbeline systems?"

To my reply, "No problem, but when?"

Came the response, "Now. Go to Stansted, the plane is waiting for you." I rushed to the airport to be met by an irate pilot, flight engineer and load master, who, very reluctantly, allowed me to board. I sat on a box with no food or seat belt and we flew in this old plane to Seeb, in Oman. I unloaded the equipment during the day in forty-five-degree heat and flew home the next day, having spent the night in a hotel in Muscat, sharing a room with two Arab gentlemen! Here was my first visit to the Middle East.

I visited Oman many times in the early seventies in an engineering role and certain other activities, good but dangerous times, taking an active part, which entailed being in army uniform and in the front line! The local British Colonel asked what rank did I want but when I said, "Brigadier," he said, "Captain will do." And a suitable uniform was provided. Enormously interesting experiences for me and a huge learning curve.

During one visit to Oman and whilst I was in uniform, I was deployed on Sarfait on the Yemeni border for a number of days and which was under regular mortar and rocket fire. For this they presented me with a local Omani medal which I gather was awarded to all officers being under fire for more than twenty-four hours.

During the redesign of Cymbeline, first a cold trial, then a hot wet trial was planned. Cold came first in Canada at a place called Shiloh, the Canadian Artillery School, about hundred miles west of Winnipeg, near Brandon, for a period of two months. All British Army and Chris Bassett from Royal Radar Establishment (RRE), now Royal Signals Radar Establishment (RSRE), with two Cymbeline systems. One system worked twenty-four hours a day in temperatures of about -45°C. I was the only civilian from EMI, supported by two REME and the gunner trials team from Larkhill. We all flew out on a C130 from Lyneham via Ganda, my first flight on a plane, although I kept this to myself. We worked our nuts off in hellish conditions to keep things working to make the trial a success, which it was. Before we left, I played ice hockey with the Brits against a US team from Minot, what a painful laugh! The Technical Director from EMI, Ron Newham, visited to wave the flag and did an excellent PR job. At the end of the trial, I had a call from Corris, who said he wanted me to take equipment, a Land Rover, and four soldiers to the US Artillery School at Fort Sill in Oklahoma to provide a firing demonstration, he would organise transport and meet us there. What a challenge, about two weeks later a bloody great C5 Galaxy turned up at Winnipeg airport to pick us up! The loadmaster said to me, "Who's in charge, bud?" And made me sign for an enormous amount of fuel, we never did get the bill! The demonstration went well but we never made a sale to the US, they cheated! We flew back to Winnipeg and then a C130 back to Lyneham after a fantastic experience and

I had actually visited the Pentagon and got a special US visa for life!

Over the coming years, I demonstrated Cymbeline at over 30 Artillery Schools plus many other sites in South America, the Middle East, Yugoslavia, Scandinavia, Europe, Central Asia, SE Asia, Africa, China, Australia and New Zealand – basically all the world, excluding what was classed then as the Eastern Bloc. Many of the territories, I visited many times, often supported by British Army personnel, or, on rare occasions, an EMI engineer. My very good friend, Andy Anderson, was quite often with me, as was Bernie Watts, an ex-gunner sergeant and Corris if a sale was imminent.

Another great experience was when the UK-Defence-Sales organisation set up a floating exhibition of defence hardware on an RFA ship (Royal Fleet Auxiliary) to do tours and firing demonstrations in friendly countries. The first was to Venezuela, Peru, Columbia and Ecuador. The Army sales teams went with the ship and company representatives flew to each country and waited for the ship to arrive – all great fun and a fantastic experience. Further similar tours were organised to Africa, the Middle East, South East Asia and South America (again), in coming years. Fortunately, I went on every tour. This great marketing experience is expanded in later chapters.

The hot wet trial (a repeat of a failure in Australia some years earlier, where I had not been involved) was organised to take place in Singapore and Malaysia. I went with Andy and the trip lasted two months. Initially, we went to Singapore, living in the Officer's Mess at Terror Barracks – well this was new, sleeping with no air-conditioning under mosquito nets. We were there for about three weeks during which time I got sunburnt playing golf with no shirt on and then drove off to the Malaysian jungle for firing trials. We camped at a place called Kidney Hill and I do mean camped; I am not a tent man in the jungle in the pissing rain but Andy loved it.

After the fourth day in the jungle, I said to Andy, late one afternoon, that I was going to drive to Malacca (about seventy miles) to a hotel and he said, "Whatever for?"

I said, "To find a decent toilet, take a bath, get a beer and some dinner, I'm fed up with jungle living!" Well of course he came with me and it was wonderful to find a proper toilet, a bath, decent food and a few beers – we then drove back!

A couple of days later, a weird event to relate, to say the least. A close family friend used to be a rubber planter in Malaysia and his last estate was the Diamond Jubilee, quite close to our jungle camp, so Andy and I set off in the evening to meet the new manager. We followed some signs in the pitch dark and pouring rain until we came to a road block with armed natives who spoke no English. Reluctantly, they walked with us up the track to the manager's bungalow and I knocked on the door. A charming lady answered and I asked for the manager by name, only to find he had left two years previously – a bit uncomfortable, however, as a typical Brit, she invited us in to meet her husband who immediately poured some very large gin and tonics. In conversation, he said his name was Brown and came from Greenford, my town of residence in London for nineteen years since birth! I asked if his father's name was Clifton Brown, who owned a curtain shop in the High Street to which he said, "Yes." Couldn't believe it, my mother used to sew curtains for him as a part-time job, what a fantastic coincidence!

Now EMI had purchased a long wheel-based Land Rover to primarily undertake overseas demonstrations where spares and tools would be carried and a Cymbeline equipment towed behind. Andy and I did a number of sales tours, the first to Iran, Kuwait, Qatar and the UAE which were quite eventful. We flew into Tehran in a C130 with the RAF as usual, stayed about two weeks, which involved events such as being shot at, having to repair the Land Rover gearbox (which I knew inside out by now) and being arrested for a motoring accident and put in jail. The latter included my passengers Andy, Corris, as well as me! Whilst in the cell, Corris commented, "Well, this is career limiting!" They did release us after about twenty-four hours, quite an experience which culminated in me attending court charged with: speeding, jumping a red light and dangerous driving, all of which was bullshit. I said 'sorry' on the advice of the embassy and was fined ten pounds. We flew on to Kuwait, followed by Qatar and Abu Dhabi, supported by four British Army sales team soldiers doing firing demonstrations in each territory, a good learning curve but with no resulting sales.

A sales visit was planned to Rio, Brazil, which proved very interesting. My Mum told me that she had known someone connected with Rio from days when she was a member of the Women's Institute in Bourne End. I explained that Rio was a very big place but Mum insisted I would meet the husband of her friend as he worked in the British Embassy, had a white Rolls Royce, and was very important! I flew to Rio, stayed at Le Meridien on the Copa Cabana Beach, where I actually met Ronny Biggs, the great train robber who was still on the run, seemed like a nice bloke! I decided I would have to visit Mum's friend in the spirit of keeping the peace so took a taxi to a downtown tower block and the lift up to the penthouse apartment and there rang the bell. A lady opened the door and said, "You must be John Sellens, your mother told me you were coming, come in and have a gin and tonic." We talked until her very smart husband came in, changed his clothes and joined us! I asked him if he worked at the British Embassy but in fact he was Chairman of Rio Tinto Zinc – he did have a white Rolls Royce, in which we drove to dinner.

A visit was discussed to take a system to Finland for assessment although DTI approval was doubtful. It was agreed and I initially went for two months, taking the Land Rover and equipment on a ferry from Purfleet on the Thames to Kotka, a four-day journey and in Finland the temperature was -20°degrees C. This visit was testing as the Finns are very technical and ran a comprehensive trial at a number of locations, including Niinisalo, Riihimaki and Rovaniemi in Lapland. What an experience and I made many, many friends along the way, particularly within the Artillery. I got to know the sauna and whilst it nearly killed me, did jump into an ice hole, what an experience. These friendships have continued and strengthened over the years and I made lots of visits to Finland on business and as a guest of the Artillery for summer and winter camps over the years. I found the Finns to be a fantastically hospitable people and they have a special place in my heart. As a bonus, we obtained a sale!

Bernie Watts and I made a sales visit to northern Norway driving from the UK and taking the ferry from Immingham, initially to Oslo, and then for the firing trials at Jurkin, near Dombos in the north, a very cold place. Corris joined us and things went well, another tough visit but successful, and a major order was won. The drive and ferry journey back to the

UK was quite eventful! We set off on the journey across Norway to the UK with two days to reach port of embarkation at the docks at Stockholm, in Sweden. This was about 1500 km, Bernie and I were to share the driving, the vehicle being the EMI long wheelbase Land Rover full of equipment and towing the one-ton, two-wheeled, trailer with a Cymbeline Radar on board. Bernie was still a serving gunner sergeant at the time and refused point blank to drive, saying it was all too valuable a cargo for him to risk. What to do, but for me to drive the full distance with no sleep, the temperature was -20°, so with snow and ice, the road conditions were dangerous. We neared the outskirts of Oslo after I had driven all day and Bernie said he knew some people in Oslo and would like to call by to say hello; I reluctantly agreed, mainly to stretch my legs. We eventually found the place at about 2200 hours and off went Bernie into the snow saying, "I won't be long" – he came back fed and watered at 0330 hours, I was very cold and very furious! The drive continued for the rest of the night and most of the next day, with me driving all the time in terrible road conditions until we reached the docks (about 600 km from Oslo). We then had to clear customs, no easy task with military equipment. However, we boarded the ferry to Immingham! I was completely knackered. Bernie was sea sick as we pulled out of the harbour and confined for most of the evening to our cabin. I managed to eat, drink and be merry until the early hours, what a wonderful and memorable night I had! We arrived at Immingham port in the late afternoon then, after more painful customs, the long drive home (another 350 km or so). What an experience! My arms ached for days as the Land Rover had no power steering but all ended well. I subsequently visited Norway on many occasions.

On a particular visit to the north of Norway, right on the coast, I had a spare long weekend and decided to drive to Rovaniemi, in Finnish Lapland, to visit some friends. On the map, it looked like an easy drive up the fjords, how wrong I was. I set off and 750 km later, arrived in Rovaniemi, a wonderful scenic drive, second to none, and in twenty-four hours of daylight as well. The views and wildlife in this desolate place were unique and once in the snow of Lapland, it was equally wonderful, the only issue was to drive back two days later.

As a test, Corris suggested that I take on Yugoslavia (as was) as a sales project as another learning curve, but not expect to win an order as the DTI would possibly not issue an export licence. I visited every month for about a year and we were finally invited for contract negotiation. Corris, Brian Wilson and Keith Bell made up the team. Brian, Keith and I actually visited a company, Rudi Cajavec in Banja Luka to review manufacture under licence opportunities. This did not happen to prove successful. During the contract negotiations, I fell ill with a kidney stone and Keith had to fly with me to the UK, first having to drop my trousers in the departure lounge for a doctor to inject a massive pain killer. Keith almost carried me onto the plane, telling the crew that I was drunk!

The marketing effort into Saudi Arabia was quite different as the package of Cymbeline systems was part of a major artillery package being sold by International Military Sales (IMS); a UK MOD operation based in London. I worked well and closely with IMS and made many visits to the Kingdom with them and a significant order was won. A lot of effort but very rewarding and proved yet again that personal relationships really matter in successful business.

A major demonstration of Cymbeline was arranged for Greece and I flew out on an RAF C130 with the equipment, the EMI Land Rover and a British soldier from the Larkhill sales team. All good until we landed at Athens International Airport and the aircraft taxied to a remote part of the airfield and opened the back door and dropped the ramp. I drove the equipment out, the doors shut and the aircraft taxied away and took off, leaving me high and dry with a junior soldier! What to do? No clearance, no immigration, bugger all. Finding a gap in the fence, I drove into Athens, found our hotel and booked in and put the soldier with the equipment to stand guard. I guess overall not one of my best decisions and the shit hit the fan from the Military Attaché at the embassy, a Brigadier, Gregor MacGregor of MacGregor Bart! He complained to London that I was irresponsible and endangering MOD property and lots more. Corris had to fly out and somehow fixed the issue, to this day I don't know how. We did the demo firing trials, another story, and the Military Attaché would not attend! It had been arranged to drive back to the UK which was an epic journey. First the drive to the port of Patras, ferry to Brindisi on the boot of Italy, then the drive across Italy, through Switzerland, in the snow, through France to Calais, ferry to Dover and home. This was all done in two days, with no sleep, passing customs using a carnet and arriving back on Christmas Eve, what an experience and no sale ever achieved!

Corris had been discussing the possibility of marketing Cymbeline to the Iraqis and had the green light to try from

DSO (Defence Sales Organisation, in Soho Square) although, if successful, a formal export licence would need to be obtained and this seemed unlikely. Not to be put off, Geoffrey decided to give it a go, which is the sign of a genuinely dedicated salesman, and with a great, world beating product.

Through diplomatic channels, two senior Iraqi officers were invited to the UK for formal presentations and to see firing trials at our Artillery School at Larkhill. The visit was planned to last five days and the hotel bookings were made at EMI expense and the two officers were collected at Heathrow, driven into London and checked-in.

As a sales engineer I was involved with the overall visit primarily to assist with the administration and act as a friendly taxi driver but to get to know these key military men. The visit went well and I learned so much, looking back, Geoffrey put a lot of trust in my ability to work with the military even though I was a civilian at heart but I had gained a lot of experience in Oman sometime earlier. I went to collect the officers from their hotel on day five of the very interesting and positive visit and drive them to the airport. I was expecting to pay the bill for four nights for two people, including breakfast, but the bill presented to me was enormous, including lots of food and drink during the night, many long-distance international phone calls and ladies for entertainment every night! I decided to pay with no questions asked, using my personal credit card and just kept smiling and hoping underneath that EMI would refund me and I had done the correct thing!

This was a serious export learning curve, make sure in advance what guests can sign for at a hotel when the company are funding and put limits in place where necessary. Geoffrey was very understanding, telling me it was the right thing to do and to pray we get an order. I got my full refund and had learned a lesson.

At the airport, we said our friendly goodbyes and the General extended his hand with something in it, was it a gold watch – in fact it was a new packet of coloured contraceptives, I looked at the General and no smile, so I said, "I will put those to good use General." There was no other word on the subject. He then said, "See you in Baghdad, Mr John." Was this an indication that we had made a sale?

Time went by and with a lot of help from DSO and the local British Military Attaché, things were looking good to achieve an order and Geoffrey made a visit to Baghdad for detailed discussions with the end user, followed by the procurement director. On his return, not much was said at my level on the chances of success but Geoffrey did tell me the decision hinged on an export licence being approved, which, at the time, he doubted. However things went well and after many months and another visit to Baghdad by Geoffrey, an order was agreed for twelve systems, plus all the relevant support equipment. This in itself was a fantastic achievement, but no one could have guessed how big a breakthrough this initial order would prove to be.

Geoffrey called me into his office sometime later and said he had a major challenge for me, which was of paramount importance to the company! He wanted me to fly to Baghdad and run a training and commissioning exercise with the Iraqi Artillery as part of the equipment supply contract. The visit would be for five weeks and be grim in all respects! Would I volunteer to go? I agreed.

My First Visit to Baghdad

Geoffrey had painted a grim picture of Baghdad but being a little naïve, I thought it could not be that bad. However, I would prepare as best I could and got a booking at the Baghdad Hotel, the only international hotel in the early seventies. Obtaining a visa was another initial epic and after many hours in the London Embassy, I had the visa stamped in my passport. It was now all systems go for the visit.

This was about 1974, not really knowing what to expect, I flew to Baghdad, arriving at a very basic international airport at around midnight. Not a quick immigration procedure but through the formalities eventually and into a taxi to the hotel which was on the banks of the Tigris River. All seemed okay and I produced my telex confirmation of the room booking only to be told, "No rooms; get out!" I spent a while trying to fix the problem but clearly there was no chance and was out on my ear, what to do! Another taxi delivered me to a very downmarket doss house, it was without air-conditioning, the bed none too clean but at least the room door had a lock on it, overall grim, so Geoffrey was correct after all!

I was up at 0800 with little sleep and decided to get a taxi to the British Embassy, where I was shown into the Defence Attaché's office. His first question was where are you staying? He must have thought what sort of pratt have EMI sent me when I told him I did not know. However, he called for his car and drove me around the city until I fortunately recognised the doss house, collected my bag, paid the bill and went back to the Embassy. I stayed at the Attaché's house for the next week, what a great guy.

I had not yet seen any of the draconian activities of Saddam's iron rule of the country, this would come later. However, initially off to army HQ to get the training and equipment commissioning underway as soon as possible. It took three days to get in and be seen by artillery officers; what a real pain, and causing my visit to be extended as the contractual requirement was five working weeks at six days a week. The plan was finally agreed and I was told that a driver would collect me from my hotel (now the Baghdad Hotel!) at 0430 hours on the coming Saturday, so a full week was lost! Actually a good achievement by Iraqi standards and without doubt, patience was a virtue; it also helped having a friend at General level (the friend made during the London visit).

Looking back it was crazy of EMI to send one man to do this job, for personal safety reasons, if nothing else, but cost savings were always a priority and knowledgeable staff another key issue. This order was thought to be a one-off and just needed the terms and conditions of contract to be met in order that the performance bond could be released (think it was ten or fifteen percent of contract value).

Whilst waiting to start the real work I went walking around the city to explore, perhaps not the safest thing to do but interesting. I found the British club, an old club pretty scruffy looking with an old snooker table, a big garden with tables and chairs, a restaurant plus beer. The food was grim but the beer good and plenty of white expat faces and to a degree a sense of safety, certainly a false sense of security. I joined immediately, having been proposed and seconded by complete strangers on day one and was issued with my membership card with passport photograph. On my return to the Baghdad Hotel, I found that the room had been searched, not covertly as you would expect but the contents of my suitcase were tipped out on the bed, all par for the course.

The Saturday came and a jeep (Russian) and driver turned up at 0430 hours on the dot and we set off for the Artillery School. The driver spoke no English so I just sat in the front seat and watched the countryside pass by, not knowing what distance we had to travel; it was in fact 200 km. The jeep was basic with no suspension, no air conditioning and very uncomfortable. This would be my everyday life for six days a week for five weeks, 400 km a day round trip and in the late afternoon temperatures of 50°C, oh my goodness, Geoffrey was right; grim, grim, grim. Now, to plan the training and commissioning but, where was the equipment? The Colonel in charge, who was a nice guy, said that all the equipment was at the airport, I would need to identify everything, get it transported to the camp and checked, item by item, THEN the work could commence! The airport cargo area had to be seen to be believed with boxes and products strewn over about two acres and the temperature was 50°C plus. The identification of everything took about two days, then it was transported the 200 km to the Artillery School. There, I opened all the boxes, ticking off each item in front of witnesses. Having lost two weeks, the real work could now start.

Each radar system had to be tested and commissioned, so, with about twelve students, I amalgamated the training and commissioning for the full team. Most were Warrant Officers, one or two were sergeants; in addition, there were two officers. The officers were fairly useless and kept disappearing for hours or days on end but what to do! Not much English was spoken, so trying to train and instruct was a nightmare. It was very hot, the facilities poor and the food

47

beyond belief. An upset tummy nicknamed 'Baghdad belly' was continuous – thank goodness for Lomital, a drug which I had to take almost every day to keep control. The camp was huge with thousands of troops, being marched and trained in many activities with numerous types of vehicles, tanks and missile systems, the colonel said, "Please don't look, this is all secret!"

Due to the delays, which were beyond my control, my visa had to be extended as it was only valid for one month (28 days), a lengthy rigmarole ensued but finally done, then to apply for an exit visa – all painfully difficult but that was the process in Iraq.

At the end of the training and commissioning, I had to write a report on all the students but was told by the colonel that the two officers must come top, a real diplomatic issue but somehow resolved. We all parted as friends, with much more to come, but I was not to know this at that stage. I flew out, not realising that many more visits to Iraq were ahead but I now had many friends in the military.

After my visit, the DA wrote the following to my boss, Geoffrey Corris: "I was most impressed with John Sellens. He could not have come out at a worse time. The weather was extremely hot, averaging around 50° and he had a daily round journey of 400 kilometres to and from the ranges. This must have been most unpleasant, sitting as he was in one of the Russian jeeps. He strikes me as being a most level-headed, sensible person who is able to adapt himself and work under conditions that many other people would refuse to accept. In discussion with him, it is also fairly obvious that he went down very well with the Iraqis and they have grown to like and trust him. He also seems able to put up with the many frustrations and difficulties one faces here. He certainly has been a credit to EMI and his conscientious and hard-working attitude has impressed me very much, signed British Defence Attaché Iraq, 1974."

Much resulted from the DA's confidence in me and my future activities in many territories which I am not permitted to discuss and my long-term association with the security services.

Iraqi Training in the UK

As part of the Cymbeline contract, commissioning and training had to be completed in-country with a duration of five working weeks, plus a full two months technical training in the UK. I had completed the in-country element and the training in the UK was managed by the Cymbeline product group based at Hayes in Middlesex, EMI's main base and headquarters. The training team for the Iraqis consisted of six or eight engineers, each specialising in specific elements of the complete system. However, none was overall expert in the complete workings of the system and if asked to deploy and operate in a combat scenario, would fail totally. My opinion is that this limited understanding was a major weakness in the support group training ability in the early days but it was addressed sometime later.

I am glad that I did not have to participate in this basic training and only got involved with visits to the British Artillery School at Larkhill, near Salisbury, to witness deployment and actual firing. Most of the Iraqis were known to me from my activities in Baghdad about one month earlier.

All were very pleased to see me and certainly viewed me as a friendly face amongst so many strangers. For the visit to Larkhill, all were in uniform and very smart but scared to put a foot wrong, which, if reported, could have significant consequences for the individual. This could include beatings, demotion, prison, and even death for them, so the fear factor was ever present (Saddam's influence) and I was seen as a fair and positive ally by all the team.

The Iraqi team were generally engineers, plus some of the Warrant Officers (WOs) who I trained in Baghdad, headed by the same useless artillery Captain. I advised the Cymbeline support manager that, at the end of the training, when competence certificates were issued, the officer must come out best in class! The consequences of not doing well for any of the Iraqi team, who had been selected as the cream from the artillery, were horrendous, as the rules were very strict, draconian and in many cases, medieval punishments handed down.

The technical training seemed to be proceeding quite well and the support group engineers organised various entertainments to get the team out to see London and some shows, all part of marketing. I looked in on the team every few days to ensure I was seen as the key man, which I hoped would help when I revisited Iraq, which, little did I know, would be many, many times over the coming months and years. I asked the guys over a tea break how things were going and if they had everything they needed, the answer came back not bad but they did want to meet girls.

The guys did not want professional ladies of the night but wanted to know how to meet local girls as friends for a good time. After a lot of deliberation and having told them I would see what I could do, I organised a night out to Hammersmith Palais, the Mecca of all Meccas (excuse the pun) and against senior advice, a mini bus was arranged and the evening set up. What a night, initially all sat at a table very subdued talking and drinking beer but looking at the many girls and wanting to dance. In the end, I stepped in and went to a table of about ten girls and said, "Would you like to dance with some Iraqi visitors?" Amazingly, they agreed and they all came and joined us, they proved to be nurses from the local hospital on a night out. What a success story and they teamed up for many more nights out on a one-to-one basis, I could walk on water (!) and was the friend of the group for life. The things you do to make friends but its friends that make life tolerable and productive.

I had to make other overseas visits during the two-month training period but still kept regular meetings with the Iraqi team, which went down well. Towards the end of the training, we had a visit by the key general (my good friend) and a colonel to check that all was well and all the contractual requirements had been met. I decided to organise a night out, and against advice from EMI, arranged a dinner for everyone at my house; much to my wife's concern as she was doing the cooking and what to have as they were all Muslim? Plenty of beer and a 26 lb turkey, with lots of side dishes, and a mini bus to bring the full team and senior visiting officers to my house, which was about twenty-five miles from their hotel, the scene was set. On arrival, I met the bus and all the team outside, many could not speak English so I advised the general that I had a very dangerous and vicious dog, it would be chained up in the kitchen but if he should get loose to all, stand very still as he was trained to kill. The general translated the message and it is true to say they were all terrified, including the general. As we walked to my front door, I said to the general that the dog was small and only trained to kill Warrant Officers; he smiled and we continued into the house and they all stood to attention, stock still, and I said I would bring the dog in so they could see it was alright but not to move as it might slip its chain. I brought my little dog in (a border terrier), very tame and it sat at my feet. The general made everyone walk over and stroke its head; he thought it a great joke and then everyone was very happy and drank beer and relaxed. The evening went very well; the food was all eaten, the turkey was a great success and I think it was stripped to the bone and a vast quantity of beer drunk.

This proved to be an excellent PR exercise as foreign visitors feel that if you invite them into your home, you consider them friends; it is not the company entertaining but personal. Over the years, I invited many visitors to my house for a drink and sometimes dinner, but usually the latter was at a local restaurant.

The technical training continued and was finally completed and I was formally invited to the final ceremony where certificates were awarded to everyone, suitably worded and the useless officer was impressed with the words stated for him as the team leader. The product group had done an excellent job and the A4 sized certificates looked very impressive. Additional presents were given to everyone to mark what was quite a historic and successful visit and much enjoyed by all.

This visit went a long way to help secure further significant business with this customer for the Cymbeline Mortar Locating radar system in Iraq and the team were my friends for life, although subsequently many were killed in the various military actions.

More Visits to Baghdad

Iraq featured very high on my priority list of visit programmes even though I visited other countries at this time due to the sales and marketing effort by Geoffrey Corris. However, the Iraqis needed help and they just might buy more systems. I started to visit almost every month, staying about a week or more, depending on what help was required. It was such a pain getting a visit visa, which was never multi entry, although this was possible in theory. It took days, with hours of waiting, and each application took about a week if you were lucky.

My second visit was a little less grim but still entailed the 400 km daily round trip to the Artillery School, plus visits to other strategic camps. This enabled me to see much of the preparations and training for war, which was of particular interest to our Defence Attaché as he could not gain entry to any of these secret areas. I spent a lot of time with the DA and most Fridays (the Iraqi equivalent of our Sunday) and Thursday evenings at the Embassy for various activities, films, BBQs and plenty of wine and beer.

Training was more of an operational nature most of the time and providing demonstrations to senior officers on various firing ranges in different parts of the country. This caused me to travel a lot by a bloody Russian jeep with a faithful driver. The jeep broke down regularly due to the high temperature, which caused the fuel pump to stop working –

the cure, pouring water on the pump. These journeys were excruciating but at least I had almost total access to all sites and installations. I stayed at various hotels, in Baghdad all of which were very poor quality, the food grim and I would class them all at one star. However, at this time, to be honest having any room was a bonus.

It was around this time that I was involved in an incident, which was life threatening, but I managed to get myself to Saddam's hospital, the Iban Sina, which was manned by expat doctors and nurses. I was in the hospital for two weeks and after surgery, was able to be discharged, once the bill had been paid thanks to the British Embassy. I then stayed with the DA's Staff Sergeant, Les Mardon, and his wife for a few days before flying to the UK with a New Zealand nurse to care for me. All quite an experience and another of my nine lives gone, but alright in the end and as always, I lived to tell the tale.

My meetings in the Iraqi Ministry of Defence were very regular and long drawn-out affairs with much tea drinking and sitting around. However, it became certain to me that more equipment was required and budget was available. I reported this back to the HQ but was disbelieved by most except the key man, Geoffrey Corris.

I completed another training course, lasting four weeks, primarily related to operational deployment and use. On completion I started to write a report on each member of the team but was told my report on the senior officer (the useless captain again) was incorrect and he was outstanding. Not a good situation, so I went to see the colonel to explain the difficulty. I found a soldier hanging by the wrists with feet off the ground in the colonel's office, badly beaten and semiconscious! The colonel said this is what happens if you don't do what you are told; this was a massive threat!

During these many regular visits, the friends I had initially made, and others made along the way, proved very useful. However, no one would meet me outside work or invite me to their house to meet family; although they wanted to, this was taboo. Two officers invited me for dinner on one occasion but needed written permission and it was not a comfortable experience; the Bath Party rules were always present and freedom very limited. I met the Brit who was arrested for bribery whilst I was in the British Club one day, he worked for a Fire Fighting Company, manufacturing fire vehicles and was the Managing Director; he got fourteen years and served the full period! I do not know if he was guilty or not but you have no rights whatsoever. Bribery was not something to do even in a mild way like hotel reception for a room or the telephone operator for an outside line quickly, absolutely never as every other person is likely to be a police informant.

On another visit, whilst in the Defence Headquarters, the senior artillery officers said they wanted a full-scale demonstration to many senior officers. I contacted EMI and requested my very good friend, Andy Anderson (retired gunner major), to fly out to support me and also Geoffrey Corris as I considered we were being tested for a repeat order. Surprisingly, Geoffrey did not come! It was a major operation on the firing ranges near Karbala (a very religious place) and a long way from Baghdad, but we still commuted daily. A massive marquee was set up for the visitors, a regiment of guns for retaliatory fire and one Cymbeline was deployed about two-hundred yards away from the marquee operated by their top team and me. Mortars were set up to fire in view of the visitors, Cymbeline would locate the mortar and the mortar crew would leave, leaving a target for the guns to be directed onto the target, which could be seen by the audience. The scene was set, the guests arrived in hundreds and Andy, with an interpreter, gave an excellent presentation. Now for the hard bit; to make it all work and the bloody radar had just packed up, what to do with no time to get a replacement radar system. I stood in the small tent with binoculars and with the map's help, gave the estimated mortar grid reference over the radio in Arabic via a Warrant Officer when it had fired a couple of rounds. The mortar crew left, leaving a target and I then directed the guns visually onto the target, supposedly using the radar via the WO on the radio and after a couple of adjustments, the order for fire for effect was given and the target obliterated – a complete success and a total con with no-one any the wiser except the Cymbeline crew who were sworn to secrecy. Even Andy could not believe what I had done when told afterwards, the Iraqi General thanked me for the successful demonstration in tears, saying the success had saved his life but he never knew the truth of what had happened. Some weeks later, Geoffrey Corris visited with the Commercial Director and a massive repeat order was negotiated and agreed.

With this massive repeat order secured, the Cymbeline Product Group became better organised, with more staff primarily to run training courses, many of which were in-country, which enabled more students to be trained. My visits continued on a regular basis to ensure we maintained our high-level contacts and obtained many more orders. Support staff started to visit to run technical training courses so I was able to concentrate much more on sales.

I found the overall position with the everyday Iraqi relaxed but they would never become too friendly in case they were investigated or being spied upon. As an expat having significant access to secure areas ensured that I was watched very closely and personal safety was always a concern and the 'special' police were everywhere. About this time, I was being pushed hard to appoint a local agent to 'help' us; this agent would perhaps be paid about five percent of the contract value. I fought against this very strongly, saying that our links were direct with the Iraqi Ministry of Defence and totally straight with no hanky panky; an agent could destroy this trust. Thank goodness I was believed and NO agent was ever appointed.

On one of my visits to the Artillery School, whilst walking with the colonel to the workshops, we walked past a foreign radar system. He said, "I bet you would like to know what that does!" He was shocked when I said I knew and wanted to know how, so I explained that I had been walking past it for months and that it was a meteorological radar because they were releasing balloons and tracking them. He then asked me to come and look inside; it was Russian. It was basically out of the ark, very antiquated, using old technology. I said, "What you need is the latest British system, called AMETS, which is state of the art and an excellent system." When he asked, "Can you tell us about it?" I said, "Let me talk to our DA at our Embassy."

The Defence Attaché was very interested and contacted the UK manufacturer, who confirmed that they would be delighted to do a presentation to the Iraqis and sell the product subject to export licence approval. I set everything up for them and after many months, they made a significant sale, I would have appreciated a letter of thanks but nothing was received!

My regular visits continued and it was becoming quite boring, but business is business. The Cymbeline support group was doing a good job but did not have the connections to help with new sales. The issues with Iran were growing and from the sites I was visiting, it was all linked to the impending war, but the press and media were playing things down perhaps as Iraq had money to spend. I was really fed up with so many visits but they were necessary. When Saddam went visiting significant sites, you went to ground as the security was very high with armed police everywhere and not a safe place to be. Armed police and army lined the route Saddam took, with soldiers every 500 m, armed to the teeth.

On every visit, my suitcase was full, not with clothes, but food. Most local food was very poor and it was always in short supply and I found the British Club options the best around but still grim. The types taken from the UK were normally baked beans, cream crackers, cheese, spam, corned beef, tomato ketchup and a few others. These luxury items helped the evenings pass and also went well with the local beer. Sometimes the duty-free at Baghdad airport had sweet things like Mars bars but these came in boxes of 36 items so even these got boring after a while. The British Embassy on a Friday was usually a good place to get some edible food for lunch, oh joy.

In the 70s and 80s, I must have visited more than forty times, latterly by road from Jordan which I will detail later and met some wonderful people, but restrictions and personal safety were always of significant concern.

Winning More Defence Business

I continued regular visits to Baghdad, using my many good contacts to keep a personal working relationship with the artillery whilst trying to promote more significant business. The problem was the continual fear factor that 'big brother' was watching at all times, the internal pressures for all Iraqis and visitors were considerable. I was very careful where I went and when and all my personal belongings were searched on every visit, not covertly, just everything tipped out on the bed. This is not a nice feeling and I think I was becoming high risk which I discussed at length with the security manager at EMI and the security services in London. It was decided that my visits were to continue but with much more caution. I do believe that I was followed for much of the time when out of the hotel!

Around this time, a repeat order for a significant amount of equipment was at the contract negotiation stage and in the final discussion stages. This package was worth many millions of pounds and the EMI contracts manager and myself were on an extended visit to hopefully secure the order. The contract was drafted and the terms and conditions finally agreed; after about two weeks of hard bargaining, the final meeting was set up for signing. We went to the meeting in the Ministry of Defence and sat in front of a procurement board; about ten officers chaired by a Brigadier General. The contracts manager was ready to sign when the General said, "Stop!" And turned to me, saying, "Mr John, do we really need all these new radars?" My response was to say, "Well, that's what you requested." But he continued, "Mr John, do we actually need them, we trust your opinion?" This was a difficult situation. My reply was, "No, in my opinion you don't need all these extra radars but more radar main units as spares to support current radars that are in service."

He said, "Thank you, go away and put a new proposal together with the new radar order halved and additional main units as spares." We left the meeting and once on our own, the contracts manager exploded and suggested if the company knew what I had done, I would probably be fired. I replied that I could not have lied; they trusted me and we returned to the hotel and had a frosty discussion over dinner.

Over the next couple of days, we put together a new package offer with half the original number of complete radar systems as instructed and my recommendation of many main unit spares added. The overall value worked out at more than the original offer, and was worth tens of millions of pounds, but the contracts manager was doubtful that they would agree. A new meeting was set up at the Ministry for a few days later with the full procurement board. We turned up suited and booted in the searing heat of 50°C, and not expecting success. The General opened the meeting, reviewed the new package and after discussion with his team said, "Agreed." And signed the contract; oh very much joy. The contracts manager was amazed and said, "They trust your every word, let's have some beer to celebrate."

My next visit entailed meetings at the specialised workshop which was established primarily to service and maintain the EMI radar systems and was managed by quite a difficult Colonel who headed the technical team. The Cymbeline Product Support Group had done a very good job training the technicians, but the workshop was lacking general working tools and everyday spares. I visited the markets to try to purchase general tools but the options were very limited, so I advised the Colonel I would address the problem at EMI and did he have a budget, the answer was yes. On my return to the UK, the initial response was we are not interested in supplying general tools and components but in the end, an offer was made and surprise, surprise; it was accepted. The package made more millions of profit but the local Colonel was delighted.

Around this time, a terrorist group of five guys attacked the British Embassy with grenades and automatic weapons. They walked up the main drive unopposed and started firing, however, the Ambassador himself got the receptionist out through the main doors into the Embassy proper, but as he closed the big heavy doors, was shot through the hand. The doors slammed shut and we were locked on the inside and the attack continued. Embarrassingly, the Defence Attaché's aid, a RAF Sergeant hid in the safe for protection! He was later relieved of his duties and sent home. No additional injuries were sustained; the Iraqi Special Forces came in and all the terrorists were shot dead, having fired a lot of rounds and thrown many grenades. Everything was hushed up and nothing reported in the press in Baghdad or in London and the Ambassador fully recovered.

My visits were now becoming less regular as most of the activities were being handled by the EMI Product Support Group. However, this was beneficial for me as I was travelling to many other territories, promoting and supporting the product in a sales role. My training days were ostensibly over which was quite a relief and my position in Iraq was now of much higher risk from a personal security aspect. On one visit, however, I went to meet the Chief of Staff as a courtesy and during friendly conversation he went very serious and said, "When did you go to Israel last?" My response was to say I had never been and if I had I could not admit it. He gave me a long look and then stated the dates I was there and the names of the senior officers I was visiting and said, "We suggest you don't go again." I never did.

In my opinion, war with Iran was looming ever closer so I was quite happy to reduce my visit programme but little did I know what would come next!

The Big Question

During the late 70s Saddam Hussein made the decision to fund the making of a propaganda film showing the overthrow of the rulers of Iraq in 1957 and the establishment of his revolutionary regime. Money was no object and a massive budget approved. Top people from ground crew, producer and director, stuntmen, actors and actresses and support staff were recruited on very inflated fees and it was said they had never been paid so much for a film scheduled to be made within about six months.

The hotel selected for the key staff to stay at was the best at the time in Iraq, The Mansour Melia, with beautiful gardens and pools, but grim food. I am glad to say I was currently staying there on an extended visit. I was supporting the EMI Commercial Managers' efforts to secure major repeat orders for the supply of defence related products to the artillery.

The majority of filming was at a desert location at Kut, a one-horse town with no suitable accommodation, approximately 170 km to the south east of Baghdad. Most members of the film team flew into Baghdad International Airport, although some made the long tortuous route by road from Kuwait or Jordan.

The lead part in the film had been given to Oliver Reed, the well-known hell-raiser and drunk. He was accompanied by his seventeen-year-old girlfriend (twenty-five years his junior), Josephine, whom he married some years later, in 1985. He also had a heavyweight minder with him, called Reg Prince, who, I believe, was of French extraction and ex Special Forces. Both in my book were without manners, behaving worse than spoilt brats with no respect for others and drunken most of the time. Reed took pleasure in showing complete strangers Polaroid pictures of a pornographic nature of him and Josephine performing in the hotel room, strange and disgusting!

Many other British actors were in the team, all of whom were well respected and quite famous in their own right, the most notable being James Bolam of the programme 'Likely Lads' fame and the more recent UCOS detective series. Marc Sinden (son of Donald), was also a member of the team, who had arrived in Baghdad by road from Kuwait and was an enigma in the team, always taking photographs and in my opinion, appearing a security risk to the Iraqi regime; not a person to be close to; perhaps playing at being a spy! Towards the end of the filming, he was arrested, put in jail for a while, was set free on Saddam's orders and fled the country to Jordan. A lucky man to survive.

My memory of the other actors in the team is a bit sketchy after so long but I do remember Virginia Denham, a charming young lady and I think George Sweeney, a tough looking person but actually a pussycat. The absolute character in the team, polite and a complete gentleman was without doubt, James Bolam. He came to my room on a number of occasions when hungry to share a tin of cold Heinz baked beans and cream crackers and cheese, a luxury! A nicer man would be hard to meet and we sometimes walked the streets together in the early evening for exercise and talked a lot.

Part way through the filming, an air attack was made on the Iraqi nuclear facility on the outskirts of Baghdad, but due to the reinforced concrete protection only superficial damage was done. The local anti-aircraft weaponry started firing about ten minutes after the jets had left the scene. Some weeks later, a second attack was made, again at low level with alternative bombs and destroyed the plant completely. The attackers were reported to be Israelis and said to have been over flying Jordan, with permission and again the Iraqi retaliatory fire commenced approximately ten minutes after the strike aircraft had gone.

The key stunt man was the very famous, Ken Buckle, an excellent horseman and nice guy; he was supported by two additional stunt men. Their expertise was certainly needed, but due to no in-country rules, except Saddam's, a number of horses lost their lives during some of the filming because of trip wire techniques which, internationally, were banned.

The lack of manners of Oliver Reed made everyone's life a misery when he was in the hotel. His hotel room was on the fifth floor and he was often shouting and swearing at full voice or being hung by his ankles from the balcony by his minder. When by the pool, always very drunk, the language was horrendous and bottles and glasses being thrown about and complete strangers being abused and sometimes thrown into the pool for no reason. Basically if Reed was in the gardens, you cleared the area. For the evening meal in the main restaurant, Reed was also a disaster; he would always be drunk and jump onto the table and then jump from table to table, kicking plates of diners' food and drinks in all directions. After this animal behaviour, he would apologise and offer to pay for everyone to reorder; what a pig. We all decided that if he walked into an area, we walked out; it was the only thing to do or end up in a fight. This man was the best example of rudeness, bad manners and drunkenness, making all the British in the hotel totally embarrassed.

I spent a lot of time on this business visit sitting in the hotel, waiting for appointments and one afternoon realised it was September 1st and my birthday!

The film was completed and seen by the Bath Party henchmen and I believe by some outside people but it never really saw the light of day, a very expensive waste of money and to the best of my knowledge, no copies have come to light. Another example of the indulgence of Saddam Hussein.

Deploying Equipment for War

I was requested by EMI to take three Cymbeline support staff, two of which were engineers, to Iraq to demonstrate a new addition to the standard equipment, called Data Memory, which could enhance performance.

We set off to Baghdad, flying to Amman in Jordan and then a dangerous onward connection to Baghdad. This flight left at night at a random time, escorted by two Mig 21s, one on each wing tip, the window blinds were supposed to be down but we peaked! On arrival, we went to the Diana Hotel, all of two-star on the banks of the Tigris River, and settled in for what was to be a very interesting visit. In fact, one of my team had never before been abroad; little did he know what was in store for him and us all.

I spent about a week making the necessary arrangements with the artillery for the demonstration, which required actual live firing, but there seemed to be a reluctance to make the detailed arrangements. I was getting an uncomfortable feeling about the whole visit and the security was beyond belief, with police and military special forces everywhere. The Embassy were of no real help and said my concerns were unfounded; there were no issues to be worried about, typical British stiff upper lip and heads in the sand as was to be fully proven sometime later. In the end, arrangements were made for firing trials to be arranged in Sulaymaniyah, to the north of Baghdad, with my team staying in Kirkuk, yet another one-horse town and very close to the Iranian border! We set off by road in Russian jeeps for the hellish journey of perhaps about 270 km to a one-star hotel in Kirkuk. Sulaymaniyah was about 120 km east of Kirkuk on the Iranian border. I was very unhappy with the situation.

We had no indication that a radar had been prepared for the trial and I became more concerned as we twiddled our thumbs in the hotel, just waiting and waiting for some action. This particular morning, we were transported to the 'range', only to find a number of radars, not just the one that we expected, why? Then truckloads of soldiers arrived, armed to the teeth and looking ready for action, this looked grim but again, why? We were allocated a radar and fitted our new

Data Memory unit within an hour and were ready to go but no movement.

The lorry loads of troops had now disappeared, as if by magic, but the soldiers were actually spread around the area which was not desert but scrub with trees and bushes. I was shown a map and told to deploy the radars for action in positions a little short of the border with Iran, things were now becoming worrying, but perhaps somewhat clearer. The troops were being deployed for our protection. This situation was not good and I expected firing to start at any moment, but we were spared this 'enjoyment'. The other members of my team seemed oblivious to the situation and the risk; we were in a potential war zone and within a couple of kilometres of the Iranian border! I gave instructions for where to locate the radars for potential action and then the operating detachments arrived, handshakes all round and they started to set up camps and dig in with their particular radar system. We were not allowed to trial the new electronic product and removed it for our safekeeping; it was the size of a shoe box. A large helicopter landed nearby and a number of senior officers disembarked, the most senior being a Brigadier General from the artillery, who I knew, but the rest were all of colonel rank and different arms. They visited each of the radar sites and inspected the locating team and how well the equipment had been deployed and dug in plus the slit trenches in the process of being dug for troop protection. We were eventually driven back to the hotel in the early afternoon and told to pack, ready to leave within an hour! My guys seemed at a loss to have any understanding of what was going on around them and thought that the new equipment trial was just being postponed.

We packed our limited kit and boarded the two Russian jeeps, expecting many uncomfortable hours of driving back to Baghdad, but we actually went back to the desert assembly point. This was about 75 km east of Kirkuk and there we joined the senior officers and told to board the waiting helicopter; we would be flying to Baghdad! This helicopter was Russian, as old as the hills, bloody big but looked in a very poor state of repair so the level of air safety had to be seriously in question. We should not have been in this position and had been conned into making the visit for an equipment trial, it was me they wanted! We took off after about an hour, amid real concern and a lot of noise, so loud that speaking together was impossible. After about twenty minutes, we landed in the desert, all went silent and I asked the Brigadier why we had landed in the desert. Informing me that we had been shot down, we had to leave the chopper and take cover where we could to wait for vehicles that were being sent to collect us and drive us the rest of the way to Baghdad, oh happy days.

We waited in the very hot and windy conditions without incident and it was now getting quite dark and totally silent, although regular radio messages were being exchanged by the signals man. There was no indication as to what actually brought the chopper down, was it old age or really military fire! A cavalcade of Russian jeeps arrived with plenty of armed troops and we drove off at breakneck speed to Baghdad, which did not take long, as the helicopter journey must have got us closer to the capital than I thought.

Once back in the Diana Hotel, I telephoned the British Embassy and spoke to the Defence Attaché, choosing my words carefully as all our phone lines were tapped and requested we all meet immediately. This was easily arranged as it was Thursday evening (club night) so we could watch the film and have a beer! I said that we would bring a briefcase each, with passports etc., and he sounded confused but said, "As you like." On arrival, I said to the DA, in private, how and when could we leave the country, his response was to say, "Whatever for?" I recounted the events of the last twenty-four hours and my belief that a war with Iran was imminent; he said, "Rubbish, you are overreacting, come and have a beer." We watched the film, drank a lot of beer and then returned to the hotel for a well-earned sleep, but I was very uneasy.

The air raid warning started at 0530 hours the next morning, or that's what I thought it was, so I got up and woke my three colleagues and suggested we get out of the hotel for safety, two told me to bugger off and went back to sleep. I left the hotel with one guy, crossed the road and went down the bank of the Tigris River and we both stood inside a massive concrete sewer pipe; I am glad to say very dry and we waited. After a while, the aircraft came over (A4s, I thought, from Iran) and started to drop bombs and the Iraqi AA started to let loose. My two guys now came running from the hotel like rabbits with their asses on fire and joined us in the sewer pipe saying, "what's going on?"

Many buildings that we could see from the river bank had been blown up and many dead or injured were lying in the street, the Diana Hotel was untouched so we returned to one room once the bombing had stopped. I elected to walk to the British Embassy to ask for help; there were no taxis, this was a walk of about four miles. Once I had got in, I met the DA and said politely, "I told you last night; it's war." He laughed and said, "No, it's an Iraqi training practice and the planes you saw were Mig 21s." What a load of crap. At this moment, more bombs started to explode around the Embassy and the DA said, "Oh dear, you had better go back to your hotel, it will be over in a few hours; sit tight it's no real problem." The naivety of this serving Colonel, who was new in post, was amazing! I walked back to the hotel and joined my colleagues in one room and tried to ring London, but all international communications were blocked, of course.

The next morning, I walked to the Embassy to ask again for help and advice on how to leave the country; the only advice was go back to the hotel and lay low, "It will all be over soon." My regard for the British Embassy was at low ebb and went totally down the drain over the next two days with no support or assistance.

On the third day, whilst all four of us were still in the same room the telephone suddenly rang and when I answered, it was my boss in London! He said, "What are you doing?"

I said, "We are all in one room in the hotel and the bombs are dropping outside as we speak." He said he had been ringing for three days and was giving me a direct order to leave the country, my response was that the airport had been bombed to hell with craters in the runway and we had no Embassy support to leave the country and a magic carpet would be great. The line then went dead and was blocked and we were on our own, no help, just good old fighting spirit and certainly no diplomatic help.

Escape from Baghdad

Having spent three days and nights basically hiding in one room in the Diana Hotel, with regular day and night bombing, all four of us were very fed up and hungry. The Embassy had been of no help whatsoever, although other countries' Embassies were organising and setting up evacuation plans for their nationals. What to do but use my own initiative and find a way out of Baghdad and home for myself and my team.

The AA and Sam6 missiles were firing at attack planes regularly; sometimes after they had left the area some ten minutes earlier and the bombing came at regular intervals. The streets were crowded with armed troops and young children aged about twelve to fourteen in uniform and armed with AK47s and firing in the air at anything or nothing. What a horrendous situation to be in and no help from anyone.

I decided that the first thing to do was get together as much cash as possible, travellers cheques mean nothing in a desperate situation like ours. We huddled together with some beer and limited food on the third evening of the war, having pooled all our cash, which amounted to about 3,000 pounds. I had 'sold' some travellers cheques for half the face value in the hotel, which helped to boost the kitty. Now what should we do as the violence and danger in Baghdad was getting worse by the hour and we had no international or local news of what might happen next. The international airport was closed, having been bombed extensively, so no chance of getting a flight anywhere.

I was getting very limited input from my colleagues but the general opinion was to sit tight and rely on the British Embassy to arrange our evacuation! My opinion and decision was to try to get out of Baghdad and sorry to say, my colleagues could join me or not, as they wished. Of course, the big question was how to get out and where to go to with all roads having military road blocks at regular intervals. My decision was that first we needed a car, with ideally an Arabic speaking driver, to leave by road and then to opt for a direction and border to aim for where the country might let us in – we had no visas. In fact we had no exit visas for leaving Iraq even if we could reach a friendly border post. I stated that early next morning, I would go out onto the streets and hopefully hire a taxi for a couple of days, or if not, steal a car, hopefully with a full tank of petrol. Then the general opinion seemed, reluctantly, to be that we should all stick together and if I could 'acquire' a vehicle, we should try to leave Baghdad. I selected Jordan as the best destination as they just might let us in with no visas but the border post was about 450 km from the Baghdad capital. We all packed a briefcase each, nothing more, and I studied a tourist map to see the general direction for the following day's journey, which seemed doomed to failure for so many reasons. There was little sleep again that night due to continued bombing, AA and missiles going off and lots of small arms being fired into the night sky.

At 0600 hours, I left the hotel, leaving my three reluctant heroes cringing in the hotel, still thinking I was crazy. The bomb damage outside was extensive, with many buildings badly damaged, or on fire, and dead bodies everywhere, plus injured people staggering about and not many cars moving amongst the rubble. I started initially to look for a taxi but none were to be found so I thought right, I will steal a car but will it have petrol and if not, where to get some! After about an hour, I found a car and a driver and managed to get him to understand that I wanted to go to the Jordanian border and offered him 1,000 pounds (in dollars). Amazingly he agreed and further agreed to get more petrol and meet me at the Diana Hotel in about an hour. I gave him a few dollars and showed him more so he knew I could pay and off he went, possibly never to be seen again, so I returned to the hotel, hoping he would turn up as planned.

We re-packed a briefcase, each mainly with personal papers, water and any food we could get hold of in the hotel and waited to see if 1,000 pounds was enough to entice the driver back. It was and he turned up with a boot full of full petrol cans and we got in with difficulty (five into a small car and temperature in the high 40s already) and set off. On the outskirts of the city, we came to the first road block of many and much to my surprise; we were waved through and took the road to Rutba, which was the border post to enter Jordan. We continued and went through a number of road blocks, manned by army, not police. To this day, I cannot believe that we were not stopped; I can only guess that the army was in disarray and four white faces caused concern at what might happen to them if we were important people. We continued onward and I was taking quite a lot of verbal abuse from my 'friends' who thought we would have been better off staying in Baghdad relying on our Embassy to get us evacuated! What a bunch of Jonahs! I pointed out that whilst we were now on a deserted desert road, we were not being bombed or potentially shot and could see the vapour trails of the attack aircraft high above us on their way to bomb the capital and we were not now on the receiving end; oh joy and happiness. The response was, "But what about the Iraqi border? We will be arrested with no exit permits or visas?" As I said, bloody Jonahs. We needed to deal with one problem at a time and continued on our way towards the border crossing. I must admit I was worried that we might be machine gunned by a passing Iranian jet, but we were not, thank goodness.

We had now travelled about 400 km from Baghdad and my thoughts were becoming focused on the border post at Rutba and how to get through it with no exit permits. As we got near the border, our driver was becoming very nervous and animated and my Arabic was just not good enough to understand what the problem might be. When we were about two km from the border, he stopped the car and said no further; to get out and he wanted his money! What to do, throw him out into the desert and steal the car, try to negotiate or pay him and walk? I went for the last option and, having paid the 1,000 pounds in dollars, there we stood at the side of the desert road, now in the dark, with the three whinging Jonahs complaining bitterly about no food etc.

So we started to walk to the border post. As we approached the immigration post, it was obvious that it was basically a wooden shed with two or three officials inside. My decision was to walk around the post, in the dark, hope to not be seen and arrested or shot and keep going, which is exactly what we did and into no man's land.

My group of Jonahs kept moaning and asking, "What now?" I explained that it was all good, we were out of Iraq without exit permits, we were not being bombed and were walking through no man's land to the Jordanian border at Karameh. It might be 30 km or more to walk but so what? They still whinged on, saying Jordan would not let us in; all negative thinking, but we kept walking until an old bus turned up, carrying Egyptian labourers and going our way. After much haggling and paying out more dollars, we climbed aboard and stood all the way to the border with a promise to take us another 400 km to Amman, the capital, if we were allowed in! We were the only white faces at the border except a British guy from our Embassy in Amman, waiting to meet the Brit families evacuated from Baghdad. He was totally miffed to find only the four of us, but set about getting us entry permits, which he succeeded in doing after a few hours; the main problem being that we had no exit stamp from Iraqi immigration. We bought some bread and bottles of water and got back on the very old bus which I doubted could make the 400 km plus trip to Amman and set off. The journey took most of the day, but we got there, got off and found a taxi to the Intercontinental Hotel, which I knew well from previous visits. Now the next problem, we looked like tramps and vagrants and they had no rooms, but after spending a few more dollars, were allowed to use the wash rooms used for prayer and religious washing by the locals, oh much more joy and happiness.

At about 0800 hours, having had some sleep on the washroom tiles, I walked to the British Airways office, which was quite close by, and it was open. The staff asked how many in our group, expecting dozens of evacuees from Baghdad from an Embassy convoy; I said four! They also had two Frenchmen and that was the sum total of six. They advised me that a BA Tri Star was on its way to collect us, issued free tickets and said get yourselves to the airport. The six of us flew back to Heathrow; the only passengers on board and ate and drank well for the first time in a tense four days with wonderful BA in-flight service.

At Heathrow, we were met by the media who were out in force, wanting interviews, but we all stuck to "No comment." We were then met by some EMI directors and managers who seemed more worried about the lost baggage, potential insurance claims and our appearance than our wellbeing. We went home.

The end of an epic journey fraught with danger, but we won through with only our wits and good luck, plus a few dollars to see us through. My opinion of our Iraqi Embassy staff and Foreign Office personnel scarred me for life, when we needed real help, it was not forthcoming.

During this time, in 1971, my good friend Sid Wright, had transferred from Green Archer MK4 to Cymbeline where he was doing an excellent job with his wealth of experience and solid engineering background. He attended and ran most of the environment trials at Chobham, fully supported the Egypt order and over time, ran most of the support visits where a high degree of knowledge was required. He and I really were, in my opinion, key contributors to the Cymbeline success story.

Now to consider a very special visit that deserves a record of its own, India. Corris had been promoting Cymbeline for a number of years with no success and was ready to walk away but asked me what we might do as a last throw of the dice. My recommendation was to take equipment to India and do a full trial, including performance, maintenance and all aspects. He said it would cost too much, but my idea would be considered by senior management. They agreed and the ball started rolling and I made an initial visit to Delhi, travelling to the Artillery School outside Bombay and meeting key army officers. It was decided that I would take the company Land Rover, full of tools and spares, and a Cymbeline system. I also had to choose an engineer to support me, now, who would go? I selected my good friend, Peter Haywood. He was the Product Support Manager, an excellent engineer and a very nice, practical guy. The visit was planned for two months' duration; an RAF C130 was booked to fly us initially to Mumbai to return to London from Delhi after the two months. We took off in late March, very apprehensive of our ability to live rough in India and survive the two months; the actual work was an afterthought! After clearing customs in Mumbai, no mean feat, we drove to the Artillery School at Devlali, about a hundred miles from Mumbai. You have to be quite special to drive in India and live to tell the tale; we eventually did over 8000 miles, sharing the driving, using a Stanfords map as a guide (no road signs) and did the job. The Devlali Officers Mess was interesting but very basic, grim food from which we suffered through two weeks; little did we know this was the best bit. We were allocated a young man (about fifteen, and speaking no English) to look after us at all times; this was a laugh. His first task was to find us some toilet paper, after sign language, he understood and disappeared for three hours! He came back happy, BUT with one, yes, one piece of toilet paper; this was going to be a trial and a half!! The firing trials and other elements went well and then we embarked on the firing trials plus accuracy tests on a range at Pokhran, in Rajasthan, many miles away. It included four days of travel with three night stops where we stayed in the visiting generals' bungalows at the relevant army camp and ate in the mess.

The accommodation was grim, without air-conditioning or running water, and often no electricity; the food was indescribable, just awful. On the road, we drank water from roadside wells which we put in a bucket with purification pills first – the single piece of toilet paper was now well used! The stopping places were at Baroda, Udaipur and Jodhpur.

At Pokhran, in the middle of a desert with temperatures of 40° plus, we slept on camp beds in the open for two weeks and working twelve hours a day. This was the site of the Indian nuclear tests of the 60s and extremely isolated. The firing trials tested the equipment to the limit and far beyond. I had to do the deployment survey and operation as Peter had little experience of actual operation; thank goodness I knew it all. As officers we were allocated a bucket of water a day to wash and drink, on one day, a donkey got loose whilst we were out working and drank all the water; a dry day for us! Toilet facilities were worse than basic, too horrible to describe, so I won't.

The trial was complete so we had to retrace our steps to Devlali, but on arrival in Jodhpur, I told the adjutant that we would stay at a local palace being converted into a hotel. He was very upset, said it was not yet open and expensive, but I insisted needing a bath, a proper toilet, running water and electricity. I got seven rooms, all mod cons, very old furnishings (pre-war) for twenty pounds – a blessing! The air-conditioning was water running through straw at the windows! We arrived back into the mess in Dulali (the World War II British Army name) happy, with the trials complete. The trials officer told me privately he would recommend purchase but to keep it confidential, which I did. We drove to Delhi to Army HQ, met up with Corris, gave a formal presentation and flew home in yet another RAF C130.

Within two years, a significant order was negotiated with a licence manufacture agreement with a company BEL in Bangalore, a job very well done, which possibly took years off my life and I thank Peter Haywood for being a perfect companion.

A sale of Cymbeline equipment was made to South Korea and after delivery, some major performance issues were believed to exist. Corris decided that I should fly out and conduct trials to try to establish what was wrong and see if anything was actually at fault within our system. A false title for me was dreamed up, which I think, from memory, said Executive Director; cards were printed and I flew out to join Bernie Watts, who was already in country, awaiting my arrival. We were located in Kwangju, in the south west of the country, and trials commenced, which were difficult due to the officer in charge; a trials officer who was not an idiot but approaching it. Reports were generated after the trial and I left the country only to return about a month later during winter, again to Kwangju, for formal meetings, which were unpleasant. The trials officer was formally blamed for the problems and the equipment performance exonerated. In private, he threatened my continued well-being, which I believe was a death threat. The local agent Mr K B Su, known to his friends as KB, was always friendly, helpful and professional and became a long-term friend. Who knows what happened to that Trials Officer, but I would not wish to meet him on a dark night!

In conclusion, Cymbeline was a fantastic period of my working life, where I learned so much; primarily from Geoffrey Corris and Andy Anderson, plus Major Ray Shortland, the trials officer. Many others at EMI, and overseas, supported me and in many cases became long term friends, I thank them all. The equipment achieved export sales in New Zealand, South Africa, Saudi Arabia, Finland, Switzerland, Nigeria, Israel, Norway, Korea, China, Malawi,

Egypt, Yugoslavia, India, Oman and Iraq with a value of perhaps 200 million pounds. I am so proud to have played a significant part in this success story. My only regret being that Geoffrey Corris did not receive formal recognition for this UK export achievement; he was the mastermind.

Abu Dhabi Defense Force, presentations on ranges at Al Ain 1975.
That's me in the suit!

Photo shot on the desert route to Abu Dhabi, U.A.E. for demonstrations in Al Ain, 1975. Andy and myself.

Cymbeline being deployed for action

Me with the Cymbeline equipment in Malaysia

Cymbeline demonstrations in Singapore

Canada

The U.K

Malaysia

Oman

Iran

Me with Geoff Corris and the Agent

Finland – Cymbeline Equipment on the move

Finland – 300mm, the largest Mortar in the world.

Chapter 5
The Dream Job

I had a call from personnel, requesting me to attend a meeting in Head Office with a Mr David George, no explanation but I knew that he was a big player and a VIP in EMI. Was it that I had done something very wrong and I was in deep trouble? We met and he said he had looked at my record and would like me to be his first recruit into a new division called Central Marketing and I would be the Marketing Manager for all EMI defence products for the Asia and Pacific region. I was taken aback and said I would consider the offer, which would include a major pay rise and a company car! I was on cloud nine, and out of politeness, went to my boss, David Beaumont, the manager of the Cymbeline Product Group. He exploded, said I was not suitable and he would block the transfer and it would not happen; I was so upset and disappointed. I went to my good friend and mentor, Geoffrey Corris, for advice, who told me not to give up, that David George gets what he wants and 'that is you'. I saw David the following day and said I wanted the job but my boss would block it; he told me to apply via personnel formally and wait and see. I got the job and, to be fair to Beaumont, he wished me well and said that I was making the right decision; we remained good friends. I had a great office in the HQ building, a good pay rise and my first company car, an ambassador. I really did think this was the top of my working career, but little did I know that there was much more to come; ups and downs.

My first job was to visit all the EMI sites and try to understand the full range of products, how they worked and what the market might require. In parallel I had to review all the potential territories as markets and see if export licences might be granted if a product was wanted. All a very daunting and challenging task, but I had the full backing of David and the EMI board. The product range was wide with airborne and ground radar systems, electronic warfare products, marine radars, germ warfare detection equipment, naval underwater systems, bomb fuses, naval gun fuses, anti-personnel mines, night vision products and much more. Who would think a record company could be so big in defence! To understand this diverse range of high-tech products and be able to identify customers and discuss and present the specific product with confidence and assurance was an enormous challenge. Another key to the marketing challenge was the use of a strong link into The Defence Sales organisation, in Soho Square, where I became a regular visitor. This organisation is manned by civilians and military personnel and helps UK companies to present and sell defence products to acceptable customers in conjunction with the DTI. The other major keys are our military attachés based in our Embassies and High Commissions overseas and all the overseas Embassy staff based in London; the easy way to rub shoulders with a spy or potential spy!

After about two months, I made my first visit into the region, using Singapore as the hub and initially visiting

Malaysia, Philippines and Thailand; the visit lasted about three weeks. The main meetings were with our Defence Attachés and some appointed local agents or potential agents and old friends from my Cymbeline days. On my return to the UK, I had a long debrief with David and the relevant Defence Sales section and planned my next sortie; this new job really was so interesting.

My next planned visit again started in Singapore, followed by Brunei, Thailand, Philippines, Australia and New Zealand. David joined me in Australia to attend with me, a defence expo. EMI had factories in Australia, making defence products (not for export) so it was a busy visit with the boss but we did get a game of golf, which I won, not good for the next pay review. The visit went well and I guess that I passed the test of confidence and knowledge to do this important job. After another major debrief back in the UK it became quite obvious that the pressure was mounting to see results. David wanted me to locate in Singapore and set up an office and become an expat, but after a lot of thought, I turned this option down and elected to commute every month. Then David threw a major opportunity into the mix which had unlikely long-term implications.

Working in the EMI HQ in London as a consultant, after retirement from the Royal Navy, was Admiral Sir Derek Empson RN; his last appointment was Second Sea Lord and Vice Admiral of the United Kingdom. This gentleman had a fantastic war record and subsequent career and was currently working on music pirate activities and royalties with the performing rites society. I was sent off to meet him with the intention of making a Far East tour plan to key territories and use his excellent introductions with various military and ministerial people to my/our advantage. Derek had commanded our fleet in the Far East during the seventies so was a genuine VIP in the region. I took to Derek immediately; he did not talk down to anyone or use his status to pressurise anyone and I could see he could help me very much and improve my education when mixing at VIP level. We planned the first tour to include Singapore, Malaysia, Thailand and the Philippines; all travel was first class and Derek arranged the in-country appointments, where we would meet all the British Ambassadors and Military Attachés, plus the local senior military leaders and supporting staff. What a daunting situation for me, who failed his eleven-plus, was a very slow starter, and was only outstanding at fresh water fishing, and as the AVM, a previous boss, said, "Would not go places." Little did I know how Derek's influence and guidance would help me in the coming years, and not just for this particular appointment.

As an aside, I joined a Free Masons Lodge in the middle seventies in Marlow, Buckinghamshire. Whilst not an advantage in business, it enabled me to meet people who I would not have had access to during normal activities. Over the years, this link enabled me to bond with so many people in so many countries for genuine friendship, and these friendships have continued to this day. I never identified any masons at EMI who were able to assist me or influence my activities in business.

Travelling with Derek was like being in another world with VIP status everywhere. When we drove anywhere official, we had an armed escort, sometimes with motorbike outriders. Every meeting was at the highest level and I was learning so much on how to behave and what etiquette to observe; Derek's guidance was administered so smoothly and without fuss; without doubt a great man in every situation and at every level. Each evening, he wrote personal letters to thank all key people we had met that day; he said he learned this habit from Lord Mountbatten when he was his aide! I had a raft of new contacts to follow up during my next tour, both in our Embassies, and local military organisations. When we flew back to the UK, with Singapore Airways, they had arranged for the plane to be the one used by their President, Lee Kuan Yew, with an upstairs bedroom, on the top deck. Derek used this during the first leg to Bahrain and allowed me to use it going on to London; yet another magic experience.

David and I had yet another long debrief and Derek was present for some of it. What an asset from the Navy sitting in London dealing with music copying without paying royalties, although again, his high-level contacts, particularly in the Far East, were an amazing help. Derek was also a director of a number of companies, which I learned much later, and was also a close friend of Prince Charles and the Royal family; he will feature later in my book as a guiding influence in my career.

My monthly visits to the ASEAN region, Australia and New Zealand continued and I cannot imagine how many miles I had flown and in some horrendous storms and lightning strikes. David had a bee in his bonnet about Japan and I started to visit on a regular basis; primarily on the Searchwater project, which was an airborne radar, whose prime role was to hunt submarines. The man running the export side was Wing Commander Murray Barton, retired; Ginger Barton to his RAF friends. Murray and I became very good friends. I was deeply involved with the attempt to sell

Searchwater to Japan, Australia and the US. However, the problem was not the radar, it was the flying platform, which, for the RAF, is the Comet 4B, but for the potential export customers, they wanted to use the Orion from the US, which eventually killed the export potential (orchestrated by the US). A lot of effort and expense for no return, but that's the defence business gamble; time and money.

After the introductions and contacts made with the Thai Navy through Derek, I spent a considerable amount of time at Sattahip which is the Naval Centre about 100 miles outside Bangkok. They were particularly interested in EMI underwater products as they had recently purchased their first submarine although this was top secret at the time. The deep mobile target was also of interest but too expensive. This product looks like a torpedo physically but is computer controlled and when dropped from a ship does various tasks and looks and sounds like a submarine so can be tracked, it is then recovered for future training. Derek flew out on a number of occasions to support my activities.

I was now very confident presenting the range of EMI products but was frustrated that so much could not be effectively sold due to export licence restrictions and the classified nature of many of the products.

The Singapore Army and Navy were key market potential, as were Malaysia, Brunei and Japan. The Philippines Navy was more difficult but all these territories took a lot of my time. I was becoming an expert in the region.

Perhaps this was when I began to tire of this dream job and all the continued travel which would have been so much reduced if I had moved to Singapore; perhaps I should have done this, but with hindsight, I do not regret my decision. I was also getting itchy feet to take on more responsibility and be more than a Marketing Manager in a safe job!

I was asked to do a sales tour of the Middle East as a special project and subsequently had a call from a gentleman called Richard Unwin to meet in London. I only knew of this chap from Corris, who said he was a consultant and good guy, whatever did he want to see me for!

On my return from yet another Far East visit, I went to London and met Richard in his London office in Grosvenor Street, Mayfair. His opening statement was to say that he had asked to see me to offer me a sales manager job in his group of companies, I told him I was not looking for a job and was happy at EMI, however, he was offering a good package, explained his group operations and I agreed to think about it over the coming week. We finished by having lunch at Ronnie Scott's Club. After the week was up, I went by train to London to meet Richard and to say thanks but no thanks. I was shown into Richard's office and he stood up shook my hand and I heard myself saying, "I accept your offer." He was delighted, I was in total disbelief and returned to EMI and resigned. David was upset and said, "How do we keep you?" I told him my mind was made up to accept this new challenge and he conceded, telling me that, should it not work out, to call him and I would always have a job there. I told my mum and dad over a dinner at Bolters Lock; my mum was appalled and nearly had a heart attack but my dad said, "Go for it."

Chapter 6
The Move to a New Challenge

I joined the Richard Unwin International Group of companies in April 1983 as one of two sales managers, still in disbelief that I had left the security of EMI for a risky small company. The starting package included my second company car, a Rover SD1, which was my pride and joy at the time which I never expected to improve upon. On one drive home from the London office late at night, I took the slip road at junction 7 off the M4 a little too fast and rolled over into a ditch; oh my goodness, and with a boot full of pyrotechnics! No one was hurt; only my pride and no damage done to the car once it was towed out by a garage the next day. After a couple of years of driving the Rover, Richard said to get a better new car. This was the MK3 Jaguar 3.4 Litre. Wonderful, and the start to driving a number of Jaguars: the best being the 4 Ldr. XJ6 which saved my life some years later due to its wonderful safety features.

Richard was the owner and Managing Director and had a very interesting non-executive board, comprising: Admiral Sir Derek Empson (Chairman), Vice Admiral Sir Ian Hogg (Company Secretary), Sir Ian Kershaw MP and Gerald

Howarth MP (later to be Sir Gerald) what an amazing group. I wondered what Sir Derek had to do with my recruitment!

The Group was made up of a number of private companies, but the main trading company was Unwin Pyrotechnics with a factory in Joyce Green Lane, Dartford, Kent. The factory manufactured a range of military pyrotechnics and big display fireworks. The factory site was large, with more than eighty buildings, including storage magazines and a proof firing area; it employed about eighty people; it was managed, when I joined, by a retired Colonel, whom I did not take to; a little too smooth and cocky, but initially I had to work with him. The group also represented a number of defence companies as an agent for certain products in certain territories; this business was usually handled via another group company. I instantly got on well with Richard and our friendship grew quickly into an almost uncanny understanding and a complete trust, which has continued to this day and also extended to both our growing families. An incredible relationship, which could well be unique.

Richard's contacts were extensive and very strong in Nigeria and darkest Africa, as well as parts of the Middle East and Far East; this worked well with my experience and also my 'magic address book', we were a formidable team from day one.

I started to travel, selling a product called 'Battlemaster', which was an electronic control of realistic training pyrotechnics, plus other military products. The key potential markets included Australia, Ghana, Nigeria, Brunei, New Zealand, Saudi Arabia, Singapore, Malaysia, Turkey, Angola, Zimbabwe and many others; some good orders were won.

The New Zealand pyrotechnics demonstration was to the SAS in Papa Kura, the North Island base which included blowing up a car and a building with SAS personnel inside; a first for me, but I pretended to know what I was doing. There was one injury, to our agent Bob Cooper, with a close quarter small explosion, he lost his eyebrows and some hair and burned his shirt, but fortunately he was alright. Orders were placed so it was a successful visit.

In Australia, the pyrotechnic demonstration was first done at the Sydney Cricket ground, to about 200 people, military, Special Forces and special effects people. No actual sales were achieved and I buggered the electronic cricket score board due to the explosions, so I was not popular. Next city was Melbourne, with channel 7 television people, and then Adelaide, but still no sales.

After about a year, the Colonel had been let go (this did not upset me) and a General Manager, Alan Kirkham, was recruited and put in to run the factory. After that came a big move for me as Richard asked me to take over as Managing Director and run the company for him whilst he went to live in Guernsey, a new, very daunting, challenge as I had no experience in running a group of companies and a factory. I had wanted more responsibility and had got it in spades; however, Richard was trusting and confident that I would do a good job. What a lot to learn, PAYE, VAT, letters of credit, bank loans, tax, people, sales and cash flow, which was all new to me.

During my initial tenure as MD, the company and I were accused by Private Eye magazine of having people killed. Total bullshit, of course, and I thought that we should just walk away and ignore the claims as ridiculous. However, the board decided to fight it and take legal action. Not a good decision in my opinion and nearly caused the company to become bankrupt due to the mounting costs. However, after eleven months of legal activity, we won the case; on the steps of the court, the person in front was Robert Maxwell, who also got an out of court settlement. Another major learning curve.

The visits to Zimbabwe were interesting; dealing with the notorious Five Brigade, but our agent was Ken Harvey, a World War II, highly decorated, hero with the Special Forces, who served with Sterling in the early days and helped me a lot. He became another personal friend and I stayed at his house and met his family many times. An interesting book and BBC programme about Special Forces' activities in Italy during the war, entitled 'Operation Tombola' says it all about Ken; what a gentle and nice man but a trained killer.

Ken introduced me to Colonel Dudley Coventry, who ran the Zimbabwe SAS; what a real gentleman, who was such a good soldier in every respect. When we discussed the products, I was selling, he said, "What's in it for me?"

I said, "That's not how I do business."

To which he replied, "You have the order. You gave the right answer."

Now Angola was yet another interesting market which produced excellent orders, but what a crappy place, and in pure poverty. I was arranging another visit to try for a repeat order under the guise of a training visit and asked my GM, Alan Kirkham, to support me for two weeks; flew out via various pretty grim African countries and ended up in Luanda. We were met on the plane by two senior officers who spoke no English and a Portuguese major who claimed to be our interpreter. After everyone had deplaned and cleared immigration, I asked if there was a problem. The major, saying yes, took out a revolver and said, "I am going to shoot the immigration officer." Oh my goodness. Then a door opened and out came ten soldiers with AK47s, cocked and ready and we were up against the wall, ready to be shot. The problem was that we had no visas and the President was unavailable, so we were being deported; which we were. I called my PA from Paris who asked how we were getting on so I informed her we were on the way home and in Paris, very tired and pissed off. We were invited back the following week by the President and went, happy days, but yes, what a down and dangerous place.

Richard introduced me to Stephen Kock, from Midland Bank, ex SAS and very close to MI6. We became very good friends, meeting regularly at the Special Forces club at the back of Harrods. He became another mentor and helped me so much over the coming years. Stephen was an enigma and a very secretive man who set up the SAS in South Africa and Zimbabwe amongst many other accolades. He helped to solve the company cash flow issues by arranging for me to meet Midaval a Midland Bank company (our company bankers) to arrange a loan against a Nigerian Letter of Credit which was delayed but worked out in the end (an advance of 250,000 pounds).

As MD I visited the factory every Friday, when I was not travelling, to sign cheques and review the week's production and general activities. I was always concerned for two reasons (a) the guard dog would not recognise me and bite me and (b) an accident would occur. This particular day, I was in Alan Kirkham's office and there was an almighty explosion, I said to Alan, "What the hell was that?" He looked out of the window and said, "Well, shed fourteen has gone!" When I asked how many people would have been in it and he said only two, or there will be a bloody row. We ran up the field and found two workers bloody and battered, about thirty yards away from the blast; both alive but injured and burned. I spoke to one, old Ted, who told me "I'm ok, Sir, but shit I went out through the roof!" Both were hospitalised but were alright, what a relief.

We did many major firework displays, as after all, Unwin pyrotechnics was historically a firework company (originally Wells Fireworks). We won a big display for the Windsor horse show funded by an American bank. I attended as the company MD, having set everything up with the Royal Household before the event as a swan was nesting in the moat close by, which I cleared with the Queen's Swan Upper Capt. John Turk, a personal friend. The event took place and when the fireworks started, we had a major problem; twenty minutes of fireworks went off instantly; it was like an atomic bomb going off. People were running in all directions; some on fire. Many marquees were on fire, a bloody disaster which I had to deal with, but no one was badly hurt; the insurance paid up and because we dealt with the problem so well, we got the job the following year and no mishaps!

Although I had to do many small displays, I learned to hate fireworks as they are so very dangerous and accidents do happen; I would ban them totally.

Nigeria was a key customer of Unwin pyrotechnics for a number of years and bought military pyrotechnics and fireworks and the group also had a number of agency agreements to support in-country sales efforts. I had visited many times whilst at EMI, so I understood the many difficulties when doing business in this very dangerous territory. Having worked and visited more than a hundred countries, I can safely say that I hated every visit to Nigeria in every respect; perhaps the only exception being getting an order and getting paid. I would never visit again and would not recommend anyone to consider doing business in this country without fully understanding the various issues, primarily personal safety.

I won a major order for training pyrotechnics for Brunei, which was a key order at the time – a wonderful country, nice people and a significant British Army outpost. I made many visits which I enjoyed over the years and it was always a pleasure to stay there.

Interesting visits to Malaysia, Singapore and Indonesia were made, but whilst interesting and positive, no orders were received in the short term and these were desperately needed if we were to survive in the long term. My concern was correct and a full review of prospects was done as we were really living hand to mouth and without Nigeria and Brunei, all our efforts would have been for nothing; I was a worried man and the stress was continuous.

The company owned a flat in Charles Street for a while, which gave me a residents parking permit for the Westminster area; what a bonus with my office in Grosvenor Street. However, I closed the office eventually and set up in Slough, which was much more cost effective and closer to home however, I did miss London. Richard was totally supportive throughout my time at his company and even when he was in Guernsey, we spoke every day and I visited regularly; his trust in me was total but we still had an uncanny understanding at all times. Derek was always on hand and we met in London almost every week to review company activities.

I established a good working relationship with senior managers at Midland bank due to cash flow difficulties which are not unusual in small companies, again all good experience for the future and thanks to Richard and Sir Derek I was, at last, becoming a genuine MD. I did have serious concerns that I would fail this challenge over my time at this company but the decision to leave EMI was a good one and was the stepping stone to bigger things. The key to success is having a good team and leadership; how true.

Richard made the decision to sell the company if we could find a buyer; this was also my opinion as the only way forward. Astra was identified as the best option and I went into the next phase of the learning curve, to sell the company with the full support of Richard. We estimated it would take about three months and I could hold things together for this length of time. It actually took about one year, during which time if I was to have a heart attack, now was the time. Eventually the deal was done and an agreement was signed that I stay with the business, not very lucrative after all my efforts, but still a job after all. If I had been less naïve, I would have ensured that I got a better personal deal.

My last day at the factory was a real event. It was a hot sunny day; a stand had been erected with food and drink laid on for about 200 guests who were coming for a product demonstration. They included senior military officers, Special Forces, bomb squad experts, politicians, reporters and the media. All went well until we demonstrated a new anti-riot gun which fired a stun grenade (which we made). I was going to fire it but one of my staff said he would do it and I should stand to one side. The grenade went off in the barrel and he lost much of his left hand, blood everywhere and I had a very lucky escape. After the guy was sent to the local hospital and those that had fainted had been revived, I carried on with the presentation with Alan Kirkham telling me that I was a callous bastard, but what else could I do! At the end I went to the hospital and then drove home to be asked, "Had a good last day?" and "What's that all over your white shirt; blood?"

Preparing For Presentations, Indonesia

Sydney Cricket Ground, Battlemaster Pyrotechnic demonstrations

Explosion on track

Chapter 7
Astra PLC

After the sale of the Richard Unwin International Group, I lost all control as an MD and was put into a mundane sales role at Astra, very much at arms-length and with no real responsibility. I was not in the leper class but not in the inner circle of key Astra staff, basically pushing me into 'the long grass'. I thought to see out my Unwin exit agreement when I would be paid off; Richard Unwin himself had a lucrative one-year consultancy (I think it was one year). Stephen Kock, now a main board director, was deeply involved in group strategy and Admiral Sir Derek Empson, was also about. All three were batting hard for me without my direct knowledge and trying to get me onto the main board, but understandably this was causing many issues and my presence on the board could be seen as a threat to the MD's position. With hindsight I am so pleased my friends' efforts failed although perhaps my experience and contacts might have helped the company survive, however I will come back to this later. Stephen Kock did, after a lot of effort, get me a good pay rise via the Chairman but I think this also caused much upset.

Astra was initially a firework company of little significance, but the key people had big ideas to expand into a major defence manufacturer and supplier to UK MOD and for export. The main driving force was Chris Gumbley, an excellent man with a British Army explosives background, who became a good friend and boss and we are still family friends to this day. Gerald James was Chairman with an excellent history in merchant banking. These two were very well supported by Jim Miller as Finance Director (a canny Scot) and Martin Guest as Technical Director. Good old John Anderson was Company Secretary who had a banking history but was a bit past his sell by date (I think). These were the key players in the Astra story and all earned my full respect and loyalty within a short space of time.

The Company grew rapidly, primarily by acquisition after an initial reverse takeover to obtain its PLC listing. Gerald and Chris masterminded the identification of companies available for purchase in the UK, the US and Canada but went one step too far by purchasing PRB in Belgium; I will come back to this later. Key in the UK was the purchase of BMARC, a subsidiary of Oerlikon in Switzerland, based in Grantham, with storage facilities at Foldingworth, an ex-RAF World War II bomber station. The directors were achieving their dream that Astra would be a world leader in defence.

I started to work more closely with Gumbley and he began to appreciate that I wanted to run his sales and marketing for him and for the complete Group, I had no designs on his job of MD/CEO, but he had the perception to recognise that I had the experience and contacts to make it work. I moved into an office in Canterbury and after a while took on a new PA who was related to Gumbley's PA. This young lady was very smart, very attractive and excellent at her job although only twenty and went by the name of Phaedra. We got on well from day one but I wish she liked longer skirts, what a distraction when doing dictation!

Gumbley and I were really getting on well and whilst I was only dealing with pyrotechnic sales, we were becoming an excellent team. Once the BMARC acquisition was completed, things started to take off. BMARC manufactured medium calibre ammunition (20 to 35 mm) and the firing platforms which were primarily for the Navy, UK MOD and for export. The Grantham factory was vast with a lot of skilled staff and all of the infrastructure to support this massive operation. In my opinion, Gumbley and his team were not qualified to run this company and my advice to hire an experienced heavyweight to restructure the company came back on me as they thought they could handle it!

Henceforth I commuted to Grantham regularly and got to know all the key people many of whom were ex-military. The Sales Manager for the BMARC products was a retired Colonel who was good but not, in my opinion, right for the expanding group; Gumbley agreed and I was initially appointed Group Marketing Director and subsequently Group Sales and Marketing Director, which caused many issues at Grantham. We, as the takeover company, were not liked by some senior staff; Gumbley was not respected as he was 'not a retired officer' and I was 'not the man for the job' because I was 'not a retired senior military officer' – oh happy days. It needs to be recognised that in most defence-oriented companies, the sales director is normally a retired senior British military officer of General status so I was the exception to the rule.

Gumbley said to me, "It's up and at 'em John, I think that you should set up your sales and marketing organisation on the top floor at the BMARC HQ." He was right, so I drove up on a Monday morning to get the ball rolling. Remember that we were hated by most of the managers at Grantham. I arrived early as usual at 0800 hours, having driven 127 miles from home, parked my Jaguar by the front of reception in a space marked 'visitor'. As I got out of the car, a woman rushed out, shouting, "You cannot park there." No questions, just the abusive statement. When I responded, "Why not, it says 'visitor'?" She shouted that it was the Brigadier's place and he always parked there, so I said, "Is he a visitor? I think not, and he's late."

Her retort was, "Are you moving your car or what?"

I said, "Or what?" Adding that my registration number would be put up as soon as possible; it was now my place and to please ask the Brigadier to come to my new office when he gets in; he works for me. The Brigadier did turn up and, as I expected, was very friendly, saying there were no problems and welcoming me to BMARC. He confirmed he had no issues with working for me and the only issue he had was that he had been waiting for a new company car for more than a year. "We'll fix that," I said, "it will be here on Friday." He got his car and we continued to become good friends, working well together – action does work sometimes.

The next major issue came on my first formal day on site. The HR director came to my office and said, "Welcome, I have found you an ideal secretary." She came to see me later; she was almost a pensioner, no fire, miserable and expensive as well as part of the BMARC mafia. This move, to Grantham, could be the pits, so I went back to my Canterbury office. I had lunch the following day with Gumbley, who could see I was down but typically looked on the bright side and after discussion suggested why not take Phaedra, who I had already made redundant. I went back to the office, called Phaedra in to ask how would she fancy moving to Grantham as my PA; she pointed out that they would all hate her up there, how true! But wanted to know what was the deal. Making it up as I went along, I said a small pay rise, travel expenses for travel up and back, local hotel paid for four days a week and a living away from home allowance; she agreed, thank goodness, but what would local gossip say; young attractive girl working for a senior director, ho ho? I raised this with Gumbley and he shrugged it off saying, "So what, you have my backing."

So we set up in Grantham with a great team of sales and marketing personnel, who were all selected by me from internal existing staff and new recruits from outside; my whole team was about twenty-five strong, and responded well to my way of doing things and Gumbley gave me a free hand but we met and spoke regularly, so he had a finger on the pulse. Many key staff at BMARC were retired British military and they all supported the 'civilian' director fully.

About the time of the acquisition of BMARC, other significant companies were acquired; particularly in the US and Canada. This meant that the group was split approximately 50/50 between the UK, the US and Canada. Furthermore, it brought a very big range of defence products to the Astra Holdings PLC portfolio, all export sales being under my control and leadership. However, Gumbley was also key in all my activities and fortunately we got on very well and I guess many saw us as the ultimate power in the Group, not far from the truth and Gumbley gained more and more respect from most of the staff at all levels.

I visited all the companies on a regular basis so the US was like a second home, and with such a high travel programme, having Phaedra as my confidential and totally loyal PA was a godsend; what a good decision to keep her with me. She was close to indispensable and seriously hated by the old guard at Grantham, but it was like water off a ducks back and whilst I was there she was bomb proof.

It was about this time I made my first regular visit to our Washington office on Concord; what an experience for a one-day meeting, coming back the same night on a 747 jumbo. The US and Canadian overall activities were managed by Dick White, another excellent and reliable company man who reported, like me, direct to Gumbley. Fortunately, I had been given authority to fly first class at all times; what a kind, expensive bonus, but with the level of travel very necessary.

I only travelled on overseas visits with Gumbley occasionally, but they were always eventful, interesting, enjoyable and positive, we made a hell of a two-man team. I did a whistle stop tour of all the North American companies accompanied by Carol Chaplin, a director of Astra pyrotechnics, a close confidante of Gumbley and a very smart and capable young lady, good looking as well. It was a very useful business trip in many respects and included quite a bit of driving. On one long drive, we had to night stop and had difficulty finding a hotel until I spotted a motel. Carol stayed in the car whilst I went to make a booking, a very tatty place and the receptionist offered a double room; when I said two rooms, he looked at me strangely and I then realised it was a brothel! We stayed with two rooms but an adjoining door; Carol was quite frightened and neither of us got much sleep – another learning curve. Our final visit was to witness some mortar firing using our proximity fuses where we would be located in a bunker in the impact area! The first issue was on arrival at Cincinnati airport as there were no and I mean no, hire cars available, we had about a hundred miles to drive to the range and Carol said, "We're done." I went hunting for transport while she looked after the bags and came back and said, "Fixed! I have hired a forty-seater bus." When she said can you drive it, well I didn't know! But we made it to the firing range to the amusement of the US Army. A very positive visit and we both made many useful business friends.

I was becoming more involved in the political activities in London, attending many receptions full of MPs, sometimes with the Chairman and/or Gumbley and this was yet another learning curve. I had a lot of help from Sir Derek and Stephen Kock and my good friend Richard Unwin, without doubt you need good friends to progress in this life.

I had a very busy day at the office and had an evening flight reservation from Gatwick but my Jaguar was in for service so I asked Phaedra to arrange a car from the car pool and got on with a lot of work. I went into my PA's office late in the afternoon only to find her crying, this was totally unusual and out of character. She would not say what the problem was so I said, "My office now I don't have time for this."

Once sitting down she said, "They're evil up here, the car pool have sent you a crappy old dirty Escort as a replacement car and it's not right."

I said, "I don't really care as long as it will get me to Gatwick but fix it if you can." About an hour later I was ready to leave and Phaedra was all smiles and saying there is a new Jaguar outside, with a car phone (no mobiles in those days). I said, "How did you do that?" and she said, "I spoke to the relevant manager and said you would fire him unless he fixed things within the hour." How to make friends and improve public relations!

It was decided at board level to appoint Gumbley's brother-in-law as MD of BMARC which in my opinion was a bad mistake and proved to be a significant error of judgement, no relevant experience and no loyalty and in my book a snake but not my decision. Gumbley was very trusting, treated everyone with respect backed them fully and expected the same in return, this proved his downfall sometime later, you find out who your real true friends are when the chips are down as I can also confirm!

We had an issue trying to get an ammunition order for the Abu Dhabi Navy and the relevant sales manager had failed to secure the order for many months so I stepped in and arranged to visit Abu Dhabi without the sales manager and flew out there. With considerable effort I met the boss of the Navy (an old friend) and asked what was causing the delay. His answer was to say "your company is dealing with the Israeli defence force". I denied this claiming that I knew all the export activities and they did not include Israel. His answer was to say that he knew me and trusted me and I certainly thought I was telling the truth but I was wrong! I flew home overnight and went straight to the London offices where a board meeting was in progress, went in and asked, not very politely, if we as a company were dealing with Israel and the Chairman said absolutely not and how could I believe an Arab! I was so mad that Gumbley had to escort me from the meeting saying you are tired, go home or you might get fired as you have upset the Chairman. It was a Friday and I did go home. I mulled all this over and on the Sunday morning drove to Grantham and demanded the keys to the MD's office from security which I eventually got and surprise, surprise found a file entitled Israel. I went to ground accepting no phone calls and went to a meeting at the London office the next day and confronted a number of directors accusing them of misleading me, putting my staff at risk when travelling in the Middle East and dumped the file on the desk which had various communications signed by key board directors and/or senior managers QED. I was not popular that day!

On a lighter note the company decided to advertise via Formula 1 motor racing. They went with Jonathan Palmer driving the Tyrell and the Porsche sports car. Jonathan was a great guy (GP qualified) but the Formula 1 car was not quite up to it so he struggled to win. However the directors had great fun attending Grand Prix racing and spent plenty inviting guests to the Astra chalet for drinks and hospitality. It was good fun but I would question if it was money well spent but I guess it was tax deductible. The best event for me was when we flew to Spar on a private jet from Manston, stayed the night in an hotel with all the drivers before the race the next day then home again – a brief stop in a very heavy work load.

I did an interesting visit to Zimbabwe using my old contacts to demonstrate mortar proximity fuses. On arrival at the special forces base I was shown into the Colonel's office and noticed all the furniture was covered with heavy duty canvas which seemed a bit odd. When the Colonel arrived, I asked why all the canvas to be told it was because of his pet lion's claws, when I said you must be joking, he went to get the pet! In he came, a bloody great lion on a chain and the

Colonel saying that the local chaps are really scared of him, I was thinking so am I, but that's the SAS for you.

The Proximity Fuse demonstration was planned to be conducted on a firing range on the outskirts of Harare and was interesting but turned out to be potentially dangerous, I think. I had six fuses to demonstrate so we went to the range in two Land Rovers with the CO and a Major plus a few soldiers. We went to the mortar launch site and the gunners produced six standard 81 mm HE mortar bombs fitted with point detonation fuses. I said here are the proximity fuses for you to fit but I was met with a blank look and told, "That's your job." Oh my goodness. I played for time and said that I had no tools or spanners so a gunner produced a big adjustable spanner from the Land Rover tool box and said, "Will that do?" What to do! Not appreciating the potential risk, I put a mortar bomb on a box and proceeded to unscrew, with difficulty, the original fuse and fitted one of mine; I actually modified four bombs, the remaining two could not be unscrewed! With no big bang, the firing successfully took place, to this day I don't know how dangerous this operation was but we made a sale.

I was in the office in London and in came the Chairman and said, "We need to visit Saudi Arabia as soon as possible, how quickly can you get two visas?" When I said in about two weeks, he replied that this was no good; we must go to meet a very influential Sheikh in the royal family and gave me the name. I did manage the visas within two days through contacts, but wanting to know why we were to meet this man, the Chairman told me that he can help us a lot. When I told him I believed he was a convicted murderer I was told I did not know what I was talking about and who was my source of information, I could not, would not divulge this. Anyway, being told I was totally wrong, off we went to Jeddah, only to find, a) I was right and b) the royal prince was very influential but wanted to meet with Astra Zeneca, the German medical company, not us! Yet another wasted effort and going off at half cock.

I think certain members of Astra Holdings were obsessed with spooks, spies, MI6 and the black hat brigade in the defence business and were totally out of their depth knowing little but thinking they knew a lot but, who am I to say more!

It was 'out of the blue' that I was made a director of Astra Defence Systems, which enabled me to be present at board discussions at Grantham, with little influence however but, able to report on relevant sales direct to the board. I do not think that the MD was too happy at my appointment but said little as it was a main board decision possibly set up by Kock. It was interesting when Stephen Kock attended meetings; he came via my office, opened his briefcase taking out a loaded automatic, saying, "Look after this for me until after the meeting." I believe Stephen was armed most of the time!

Now we come to the investigation and ultimate acquisition of PRB in Belgium; without doubt, and with hindsight, it was a step too far. However, when a company grows by acquisition rather than genuine organic growth, it is fine until the purchase is a bad one like PRB. The board was desperate for something positive to produce revenue also I believe they were being encouraged to purchase PRB by UK MOD as a second source supplier! Gumbley sent me to visit all the PRB operations, as he had already done to 'test the water' and get a feel for what we would be getting for our money and what the short-term upside might be in sales and revenue.

PRB had a number of manufacturing sites in Belgium with the HQ in the capital. I was made welcome on every visit and transport and visit programme put together in a very professional manner. The range of products manufactured was impressive including medium and heavy calibre ammunition, rockets, fuses, pyrotechnics, propellant, electronics and much, much more. I started to visit each plant, meeting all the relevant staff and witnessing key production which was more than just interesting, however I kept getting the feeling that much was being done for show and was not regular production, perhaps I was too critical but this was why Gumbley sent me. I also thought that a couple of the sites had been staffed by rent-a-crowd. Some of the heavy shells being manufactured were of odd calibre and caused me to wonder who the end user might be! The Super Gun propellant was being produced for Iraq and PRB had a close working relationship with Gerald Bull the designer of the Super Gun and the boss of his company SRC (Space Research Corporation). All in all, I did not have a comfortable feeling, but no proof of wrongdoing, just total concern of a massive con. I reported my concerns to Gumbley and the board but there was so much pressure to do the deal and to improve revenue that the board went ahead with horrendous consequences.

I put one of my senior sales managers into the company HQ, tasked to look at all potential and current order status; he got zero cooperation and was misled all the time, as I was on my regular visits. My big concern was existing contracts where deliveries were about to be made and who were the real end users as, if not acceptable to our DTI Astra as the new owners would be acting illegally. Surprise, surprise most of the main contracts were unacceptable to the UK authorities and had to be immediately cancelled so the revenue expected from the acquisition disappeared almost overnight, this was the start of the demise of Astra Holdings PLC. I still cannot understand how we and our expert advisors accepted the order book and end user statement on face value without a detailed review and full and comprehensive understanding. The excuse by PRB at the time was they were bound by security, how could our expert advisors accept this, but they did? At this stage, life went on with a lot of effort to salvage the situation but the die was cast. Gumbley was as usual positive and larger than life and he and I went on a sales tour of the Far East in an effort to drum up some business, however whilst in Thailand, he got a phone call and, turning white, said that he had to return to the UK – immediately. The bottom line was the Chairman was removed and Gumbley subsequently resigned, in my book a tragedy but maybe unavoidable in very difficult circumstances.

A meeting of senior managers was called by the newly appointed CEO, who had already had a sales presentation from me the previous day. I stated our order book of approved export orders of approximately 200 million pounds, he said, "Not enough." And I and my staff were all lazy and I would be under legal investigation related to other matters. The meetings went from bad to worse and I decided to resign with immediate effect; picked up my briefcase and walked out. I drove to the local hotel to pick up my bag and pay the bill, but before I left, a number of my staff turned up to try to talk me into staying; they failed and I drove home and put my resignation into writing to the new CEO. In my book, he was an overpaid bum as was perhaps proven many months later when he took the company into liquidation.

I decided to go off the radar, having resigned and ignored all the calls from the new CEO for seven days but then reluctantly decided to go and meet him in the Canterbury office. It was an interesting meeting and he tried, I think, to be friendly. He said, "I take back my statement that you are lazy as you have not had a day off for a year, bad management, but your staff are crap." He then said that he wanted me to stay on as his right-hand man (I think hatchet man) as I was the most senior man with full company knowledge. I could keep my Jaguar car; have a pay rise but travel economy. I agreed to consider his offer but had no intention of accepting and when I got home, resigned again. This man had no integrity or honesty in my eyes and did not know the defence business and there was no way we could work together, ever. I also think that having the Chairman removed from a PLC, the CEO resigned and the Group Sales and Marketing Director resigning in March; the last month in the financial year was not good for the share price, investors or the city!

I arranged for one of my ex-staff to visit my home to take all my files and company property back to the company, which was good forward thinking as I was about to be raided by the police. They came at five in the morning and searched the house (not very well); they found my shredding machine, saying we have the technology to put anything back together. I told them that would be hard, I had burnt it all last week; they did not laugh. I was arrested and taken to Canterbury police station because the company was registered there but was allowed to call my lawyer first. I was interrogated for about ten hours which was another learning curve but was not charged with anything and released on police bail with passports returned. My lawyer advised that it's no problem, you have done nothing wrong; they are trying to frighten you (in this they were very successful) for information, some of which is classified; you have pieces of the jigsaw but keep saying 'no comment', which I did. Over time, as a company director who knew a lot, I was requested to attend various inquiries but for a number of reasons never did! The press pursued me for the 'Astra story', offering large sums of money but I continued with 'no comment'. The man who knew a lot never spoke! My home phone was tapped for about three months; I was followed continuously and some people tried to murder me in an organised major car crash on the M4, which I was lucky to survive, very difficult times and extremely stressful but all part of life in the defence fast lane; oh happy days. You soon learn who your real friends are when the chips are down and not the ones you perhaps expect. At Astra in the good days, everyone wanted to know me and be my friend, not now. In the defence business generally, I could count the real friends on two hands.

During further interrogation at a later date by MOD police, it was stated that I was present at the Defence Exhibition in Baghdad, Iraq in 1989 and was promoting the Super Gun designed by Gerry Bull! A model of the gun was certainly on display on the SRC (Space Research Corporation) stand and Astra Holdings Plc also had a stand. It would therefore be logical for me as Group Sales and Marketing Director at Astra to be present. The PRB links with SRC and the takeover by Astra of PRB made this almost certain but I was not in the country. The police accused me of fabricating a story and being part of a cover-up and produced a copy of my passport showing an Iraqi visa issued for the exhibition; this was actually correct but I did not visit for security reasons. However, I pointed out that if they looked more carefully, they would not find an in/out immigration stamp from Baghdad International Airport so I had told the truth. I did not attend the exhibition, was not in the country and was not involved in any cover-up, "Get back in your box MOD."

My lawyer said I should take legal action against Astra for holiday pay, my formal notice period and 10,000 of unpaid pension bonus BUT it could take a year and they probably would go bust before they were forced to settle. I speculated the 3,000-pound fee, which I had to borrow and one year later got paid with interest even after the first cheque bounced and second was not signed, typical behaviour of the new management who decimated my division with most staff being made redundant.

A very disappointing end to my time at Astra, which overall I enjoyed and was a fantastic experience and I thank my friend Chris Gumbley for all the trust he put in me and for his continued support. Richard Unwin, Stephen Kock and Sir Derek Empson were also true friends for whom I will be eternally grateful.

Now to recover, pay the legal fees and overdraft and move forward positively, you cannot keep a good man down.

Astra Holdings: A range of products

Meeting senior official at Defence Expo

FOCUS ON ASTRA SALES & MARKETING PERSONNEL

As part of the Groups plans for future growth we have now formalised the Astra Holdings Group Sales and Marketing team at Grantham under the leadership of Sales & Marketing Director John Sellens.

The new team is responsible for all the Groups Sales and Marketing activities world wide, with the exception of North America, which is handled by the Astra Holdings Corporation in close liasion with the U.K. team.

John Sellens
Group Sales & Marketing Director
After an electronic engineering apprenticeship followed by an engineering and marketing career spanning 22 years at Thorn EMI, he joined Richard Lowe International Limited in 1987 as Managing Director of Leisure. He successfully negotiated the sale of the company to Astra Holdings PLC, culminating in 1989 (in 6 months before taking up a post as Sales and Marketing. His current appointment commenced in January 1990. John is a 47 year old family man with 3 daughters and a 5 year old grandchild.

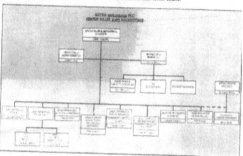

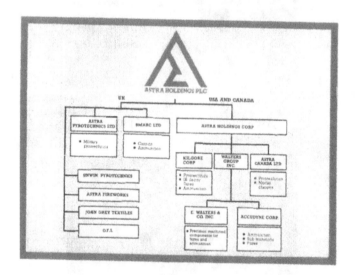

Chapter 8
Recovery

Now to the recovery period which was urgently needed as I was unemployed, had no savings, only a big overdraft, a mortgage with a very high interest rate (about fifteen percent at the time), a family to support and a black cloud hanging over me with the press and media hounding me and with personal security issues.

I was approached by Alan Evans, a senior director of a small defence company called Hall and Watts about a sales director job based at St Albans. The package was good with a 50k basic salary, bonus potential, private medical cover, pension and I could have a Jaguar car again! An offer that was not too popular with the other main directors of Hall and Watts Middle East but Alan had the power and I accepted the offer, having explained the issues hanging over me. Just before my recruitment, a retired Brigadier, Geoffrey Ransby, was taken on to head up Middle East sales and I was therefore given Africa, not my favourite choice as all my main contacts were in other regions. The whole company was predominately an old boys' network of military personnel, most of them NCO level apart from the directors but Geoffrey was the most senior which caused friction, however, although I was the odd ball Geoffrey and I got on very well. Soon after I joined, Linda was recruited as the board directors' PA but she also supported my administration work when I needed it; a very talented person, strictly confidential and very professional in every respect, she helped me a lot during very difficult times.

Hall and Watts Middle East was basically a defence agent for UK companies and worked on a commission basis with no manufactured product, not what I was used to and not ideal. My travel was primarily to Kenya, Tanzania, Uganda, Zimbabwe and Morocco, plus others for spot opportunities. Not easy markets; all very corrupt and not my way of doing business but I would do my best to get orders. A key company that we represented was Carmichael a leading fire truck manufacturer and significant orders had been secured with Hall and Watts Middle East assistance.

I got to know the Chairman of the Dubai Municipality who said, "It's a pity you cannot offer to supply us with any products." I asked what he needed and his reply was, "Waste bins!" The bins were large skips on four wheels in hot dipped galvanised steel, supplied sole source from Germany. He offered to provide one for us to copy and then bid for the next contract (he was Chairman of the tender board). The new sample was delivered to the airport to be flown to the UK and reverse engineered with subtle differences. Whilst at Dubai airport awaiting shipment it got filled with rubbish! I climbed in and emptied it in the heat of the day (45 C) and it then went on its way to Scotland to a selected engineering Company. They did the job; we bid and won a massive contract and delivered on time with some hard local assembly in Dubai. All good profit for Hall and Watts Middle East although an odd item to supply.

I was travelling quite a lot but nothing like previous years at Astra and EMI but apart from fire trucks business was very poor and even that business needed ODI aid to support a purchase. It is fair to say I was not delivering orders and whilst my contacts were strong, I was not 'earning my corn' so it was decided to bring me into the Middle East activities to assist Geoffrey. We embarked on two key projects together in the UAE, the civil project providing waste bins for Dubai and Special Forces military products for Sheikh Mohamed's private army based in Abu Dhabi. Geoffrey was also involved with some other opportunities like cigarettes, gold and others which I kept well clear of for a number of reasons.

I had regular meetings with Alan Evans and we got on well but the pressure was mounting for the company to produce revenue. The directors, in their wisdom, had embarked on a real estate/housing project in Scotland called Aldargy, which turned into a white elephant and financial disaster; thankfully I was not involved with this speculative idea. In the December of my second year I was demoted, with my salary reduced by forty percent; with hindsight I should have quit but I stayed on for about another year before we were all made redundant.

The day after my demotion, the company had a major PR reception in London, many of the senior guests invited by me; I still attended even though our MD treated me like a skivvy. I should have walked out but I would like to think that I was more professional than our MD and in consideration, could brush off this behaviour, meeting up again with the many guests I knew and with my good friend Sir Derek Empson, the most senior officer present at this reception.

I was now spending most of my time in Dubai helping Geoffrey put together various packages of SAS/SBS products for Sheikh Mohamed's elite special forces. Good revenue was secured and we sold a lot of waste bins to the Dubai Municipality, however the company was failing and in the October Geoffrey was made redundant and took it very badly, I was next to go within the hour and it was a happy release. However I got verbal agreement that if I could get the release of a performance bond in the UAE valued at about 200,000 pounds, they would pay me 25k. I took the MD at his word spent Christmas in Dubai at my expense and successfully got the bond refunded. The MD reneged and paid me nothing so I took out a winding up order and the company closed down, I got nothing in return but expense and some satisfaction. Alan Evans was always true to his word and paid me one third of the debt and another third sometime later from his personal funds, a true to his word gentleman. Now, to find another job.

Looking for a job again although I had been looking for some months with nothing positive, now the chips were truly down; unemployed and with a lot of debt as for the last twelve months my income was lower than my outgoings. Overall, and to be crude, deep shit all around.

I contacted some good friends at my old company EMI where things had changed a lot but I got an interview at the Crawley offices with HR but whilst they had a good opportunity for me it was blocked at the final hurdle by a local director. I later heard that he considered me a threat. However because of my background I was referred to Central Marketing at Hayes which was now run by Mike Penery, this was déjà vu and really going back in time. I was given an interview with Mike who said, "We do have a vacancy but I consider you are too highly qualified and it's in Saudi Arabia. Could you take such a step down, a lower salary than you have been used to and live in Saudi?" I said, "Yes," got the job and started three weeks later after my PV vetting was approved. My boss was Peter Rodwell, an ex-Plessey radar engineer who knew my background and he himself was a Saudi expert. This guy was an excellent boss and treated me with respect and understanding, he helped me so much during very difficult times and my thanks cannot be overstated, an absolute gentleman and we became good friends even though he kept beating me at golf.

What was required of me was to front all the EMI (now Thorn EMI) defence business in the Kingdom which was considerable (greater than 100 million and growing) and act as the 'corporate office manager'. I had a few weeks to get to know the key range of products supplied or hopefully to be supplied. I already knew the Kingdom well, having supplied Cymbeline and Ranger to the army during my Cymbeline days via IMS (an MOD selling agency); on these projects I must have visited about fifteen times with more visits whilst at Astra. I flew out to Riyadh in January with an overnight bag and a set of golf clubs (the latter was Peter's idea and good thinking) Annette was with me but getting her visa was an epic as I had no residence permit (egama). Then to open a bank account, rent and furnish a villa, get a car, etcetera; however, we had a very good local agent who solved many of the problems and in a short space of time I was up and running.

Peter visited often and I got to know many key military Saudis and BAE staff in a short space of time. Mike Penery and other senior Thorn EMI staff visited plus senior MOD personnel; we were very popular.

The Kingdom is a very strange place to visit or live, you never feel safe; you have no rights whatsoever and if you try to buck the system, you will go to jail, however, we never had any trouble but were very, very careful. It was always great to visit the Embassy for a reception and have a drink. Peter knew the score and advised if it gets on top of you, to go to Bahrain for a few days 'R&R' – that's just how kind and understanding he was.

At this time there was only one eighteen-hole golf course in the Kingdom, it was located near Riyadh international airport and was a sand only course. The greens (browns!) were oiled, rolled, raked and a cross rolled with the hole in the centre. You chipped on then moved the ball onto the rolled cross and putted, all very novel. On the fairway you placed your ball on a plastic grass mat and then played the shot. Not proper golf but fun and Peter and I played regularly when he visited, I joined the club.

Our first villa was on the Al Umama 1 compound on the outskirts of this big sprawling city, a thirty-minute drive from my office which was located, initially, in our agent's house. Driving in the Kingdom was a very dangerous pastime as the Saudis took little care, did not drive to the rules and often young boys might be at the wheel! This was, in my opinion, the most risky part of my job! In Saudi, you have nothing to do but work, save money, eat and think about having a beer unless you made your own wine, whatever next but we all did it, potent stuff which tasted very bad most of the time. You could buy the local Sadiki, expensive, risky and vital to know you were buying from a good batch, it had to be heavily diluted as no joke it could be lethal. Newer arrivals would be asked by other expats, "Have you joined the blue flame club yet?" But if you got caught, it could be years in jail and great creativity went into hiding places, cavity walls etcetera.

The job was challenging and caused me to travel throughout the Kingdom very regularly. I also flew out of country a lot for various reasons so this new responsibility was just what I needed after the difficult times in the UK. It was also great to pay no tax legitimately so my UK debts were reducing rapidly. This job really was what I needed at this particular time in my life.

I decided to try to get Mum and Dad into the Kingdom for a month-long holiday, which, with a lot of help from our agent and Peter, we managed. Even though in their early 80s, they had a fantastic time and our many friends on the compound were very hospitable. They came again the following year for another one-month holiday and again a highlight in their latter years; it was a blessing to see them so happy.

The key products being supplied to the Kingdom at this time were state of the art bomb fuses and GETs (ground emission terminals) the latter handled the information transmitted by AWACS aircraft (airborne warning and control systems) which flew continuously in the region. This equipment cost tens of millions, it was top secret and a small number were deployed in the Kingdom. My links with BAE systems were becoming very strong and they had more than 5000 staff based in the Kingdom supporting supplied products including Tornado aircraft and associated equipment. Perhaps I was starting to think of my next move, could it be to BAE?

I never did apply for residency and therefore could not purchase a company car so I hired a Mercedes in Bahrain.

After the first year, we changed location and rented a villa in the Saudi British Bank compound in the centre of Riyadh. This compound had an extensive video library of films which was a major benefit to pass the evenings on home brew. I have not mentioned the weather, which, for much of the year, can only be described as 'bloody hot' and at certain times of year, very humid, all in all, not nice.

When visiting Jeddah and the various places north, I would often drive from Riyadh, which took about eleven hours; most of which was totally boring but Ta'if and down the dodgy mountain pass and past Mecca was always interesting. I did this journey twice with Mum and Dad during their holidays and they loved it, a real experience.

During my second, year I moved office to work out of the Al Kurdi office which had a Thorn EMI expat working on fire and security by the name of John Robertson who technically reported to me but had just resigned. A good chap but perhaps with a bit more Scottish blood and temper than was good for him, he would feature much later in my advancement. He left the Kingdom under a bit of a cloud and would not let me try to help his situation, an obstinate Scot! Al Kurdi was an interesting company and again would prove to be of significant importance in the coming year or two.

I needed to have meetings with some key contacts in Cyprus and flew over on a number of occasions which enabled me to meet up with my good friend Sir Derek who was now living there after leaving the UK due to a number of personal issues which included being hounded by the media. He was quite well and it was good to see him again although he seemed a beaten man.

Overall, I was enjoying my deployment in the Kingdom of Saudi Arabia and returned to the UK for an urgent meeting with senior management towards the end of the second year. I was informed that the defence operation was being sold to the French company Thales and I would be redundant, another crisis situation but Rodwell and Penery offered a life line as the Middle East sales manager for Thorn Security. Not my comfort zone but a job, and the company was in the process of an MBO, and I was told that I could make some real money so I said, "Okay." The first task was to set up a new fire and security office in Dubai. I organised a forty-foot container to transport my goods and chattels to Dubai, having rented a luxury apartment in Satwa with the help of the Thorn Security agent and moved to the new location and a new challenge.

Golfing on the sand course at Riyadh, Saudi Arabia

Chapter 9
The Family

Having spent my early teens providing the music for a local ballet school that my sister attended, I met Annette Holland, one of the top performers at the same school. I travelled around to all the competitions providing the music for all the girls via my top of the range tape recorder, the big purchase from my Premium Bond win. Whilst fishing was my first love, I somehow found myself getting married at twenty to Annette, on the 22nd July 1966, at Acton Registry Office which was a shock to everyone including me, but not Annette! The reception had to be postponed as I was in hospital for emergency surgery for appendicitis after which we lived at home with Mum and Dad, trying to save a deposit for a house. This we eventually did, although it was a flat.

Our first daughter, Maria Anne was born in 1969, Claire Louise in 1973, and Tina Jane in 1975. Annette basically brought them up as I was always travelling and working, which may account for some of the troubles we had with the first two; me not being around much.

Maria left home at sixteen to live with a useless guy who fathered her three children, Anna, Lisa and Sean. Claire was next to go but came back after a while, Claire had four children, Craig, Alice, Jack and Ella Mae. Tina was more steady and married Daniel Snapes, an excellent young man and excellent father to their six children, Michael, Paige, Jade, Skye, Paris and Dani. What a tribe, but the story is never ending, with thirteen great-grandchildren last count; Maria with six, Claire three and Tina four; as I said, what a tribe to support!

I guess a very happy tribe who all get on reasonably well, but Maria is the outsider and kept at arms-length by her two sisters, which I find very disappointing but something we have learned to accept.

My mum and dad featured so much in my life and Annette's mum and dad accepted me fully into their family, old fashioned maybe, but I believe very positive.

For about twenty years, my grandmother, Pearson, (Mum's Mum, Nell) lived with Mum and Dad, which was a mistake for much of the time and a bad initial decision on Mum's part. She was a bitter and cantankerous person, very moody and quite nasty at times and as hard as nails. She said I was the only one she trusted and Mum and Dad were after her money (actually she had none). She made Mum's life very difficult but Dad had a way out by going fishing. Grandmother had her 100th birthday at home with Mum and Dad but then went into a home which I organised as Mum would not. It was a necessary move and it was better, she died at 103 of old age. It was sad that she did not have a happier time during the last thirty years of her life but this was all of her own making even though we all tried very hard to make her happy.

The new generation of the Pearson family came from my mum's brother Reg who died tragically early in life. His son

Martin and sister Lesley grew up with their own families and I am glad to say are all well and we keep in touch, although don't meet regularly.

It was a great loss when our mums and dads passed away; Albert Holland was quite ill for some time having moved from Fareham to Bourne End just before his passing. Joan passed away prematurely caused by an existing untreated condition which was tragic. My dad passed away at ninety-five and I guess due to old age, although his final years had seen him house bound. Very unfortunately, I was seriously ill in Dubai at the time, awaiting urgent surgery so did not see him at the end but my lifetime memories of happy times will live with me forever. My Mum passed away at ninety-six primarily of old age after a wonderful life. All so sad but we all have to go sometime and theirs were full and happy lives.

My dad kept fishing until he was about ninety, much to the annoyance of my mum and he fished with me in Dubai when they visited, which I will come to later. If there is a river in heaven, he will be a very happy man perhaps waiting for me to join him! Towards the end of my mum's life my sister who she depended on very much was diagnosed with leukaemia and could not get to see her due to extensive treatment over many months, we kept this from Mum although I think she guessed. Against all the odds my sister was cured but it was a very long, painful and difficult process, she is one of the lucky ones and owes everything to the NHS, a bone marrow transplant from a German and her own faith.

I had a strange meeting with my dad when he was in his early 80s; he was at home alone crying, saying he was about to die! He said he was in pain all over and this was the end of the course, despite telling him it would pass, I was worried.

Two days later he phoned me to say he was fixed, cured. When I said, "How?"

He said, "Well, actually not yet but I've read an article in a magazine which details my condition and with some pills I really will be fixed." Amazingly, he was correct; it was polymyalgia rheumatica, and after a course of steroids, he was fixed. Unfortunately, it is a hereditary condition and my sister and I have it but it has been treated successfully.

I consider overall a very lucky family group (the tribe!) and whilst I have missed much of the growing up, perhaps I had the best of all worlds.

Chapter 10
A New Career

Thorn Security

I initially transferred to Thorn Security whilst I was still living in Saudi Arabia and the company had just split from the group but retained the name although now a private company after a management buyout (MBO). Mike Penery helped to organise the MBO but did not become part of the deal, I never understood why. The company was an established leader in the supply of fire detection and suppression products and security systems; the HQ was located in Sunbury-on-Thames with a large staff. I knew nothing about fire detection and suppression but was told that as a director it did not matter! Whilst still part of Thorn EMI massive packages of high value product, primarily to protect aircraft and hangars had been supplied to the military in Saudi Arabia, I had not been involved with the supply only the support activities. I started by trying to understand the products which were supplied for export via locally appointed exclusive agents (sometimes crooks and facilitators). I made a plan to set up the Middle East sales hub in the United Arab Emirates as Saudi Arabia was too restricted. This plan approved, I started initially to establish a base with the help of the local agent in Dubai and after a lot of searching found an apartment in Satwa which seemed perfectly located. I had this apartment for nearly twenty years but had no idea at the time that it would be my home for so long.

Initially, I worked from home, which is not easy, I survived but business was difficult. I had an expat, Gordon Blackwood working for me based in Abu Dhabi who was very good and over a period of time won some excellent orders in the power sector. About this time I was in contact with Linda who had moved on to another company after being made redundant from Hall and Watts but was still looking around for something better and would possibly be interested in the Middle East so I referred her to Thorn Security HR who recruited her as my PA, what a lucky break. She joined me with the initial task of setting up a Thorn Security office to look after all sales in the region. I elected to go for the Jebel Ali Free Zone and Linda set the ball rolling while I was travelling trying to get orders in the region.

At this time, the UAE was expanding rapidly and Dubai was leading the charge; however I was looking in many different territories as well as the UAE, all of which I had visited many times and had many contacts. I now had a raft of representatives/agents for Thorn Security products and most agreements of an exclusive nature.

The main buildings being fully occupied at Jebel Ali Free Zone, we were allocated 'temporary' offices. This had the positive result of placing us near the Abu Dhabi Road zone exit gates; an excellent location as all the team made frequent drives to Abu Dhabi to maintain contact on projects there. The building was one of a small group of single storey chalet type buildings and a few other companies had an office base in ours; we took up two offices one for project work and one for sales and administration. Being rather 'out in the desert' most mornings we were greeted by some fascinating desert insect life that had found its way in, especially while the workmen were putting in extra computer cabling for us. The administration of the zone itself was excellent and we were able to do all the required licensing and visas for the company, staff and cars very efficiently. There were also good facilities for lunch and dinner, even evening entertainment, although the latter was rarely used by any of us as all the staff lived in Dubai city.

The word in the board room and to staff was that Thorn Security would go to the city within two years and become a PLC. I never thought this would happen and the real plan was to sell the company and enable all the directors to make a financial killing. This thought was borne out by the way turnover was being boosted at any price and key offices were being established in the UAE and Kuala Lumpur in Malaysia. Many orders were being secured at low margins which gave a false order book success rate if you knew the fine detail.

Kuwait was a place I visited on many occasions, both with a defence hat on in the early days and then related to fire and life safety. It is a grim and severe place and the climate unbearable; in the summer, one of the hottest places in the region. I never found the locals very friendly and without oil (which we found and gave away) it would not be of any interest to expats. The oil sector is massive and the crude storage facilities and associated organisations need to be seen to be believed. I visited within days of the finish of the Gulf war with Iraq and it was hard to breathe due to all the oil fires.

Live ordnance was scattered everywhere and the destruction and wilful damage done by the Iraqi forces during the invasion was tragic. Over the years I got to know an Indian engineer called Jose Murikan very well, what a character and good friend. He worked for a major Kuwaiti company (in the top three) and was known as 'Mr Fire' in the country. I provided a significant volume of fire products via Jose and his company over the years. I also had the pleasure of eating many take away curries in the apartment that Jose lived in for more than twenty years and his hospitality a fantastic boost when visiting. The Joint Venture (JV) that we set up for UTC sometime later in conjunction with Jose's company would never have been concluded positively without his support and assistance. Jose is now enjoying retirement with his wife and family in India and I try to keep in touch with a great and loyal friend.

This continued to be a happy time for me, left alone to my own devices, lots of travel all over the region and my golf was improving and the sea fishing was great. Furthermore, I was still tax free, oh very much joy. A key project in Dubai was for a completely integrated fire and security system for the new national bank, which was being built on the creek in the centre of the city. Very prodigious and a must win project and possibly a unique system at the time. We did finally win the order at about a zero margin and even the local representative who played a major part in our success got no commission on the initial order. During the bank project I got to know a number of the project management team well, one of which became a long-term friend. Frank Webster and his family were very hospitable often inviting me to barbeques at their villa which was always a delight. Over the years, Frank helped me a lot; his professional approach to business was respected and appreciated. His three children grew up over the years but often came with us on fishing trips in the Gulf.

Our main competitor was Tyco the world leader in fire and security, their Middle East office was located in Abu Dhabi run by a guy I would not trust but they did have a very strong and influential UAE partner who held a senior position in the oil and gas industry. Not surprisingly Tyco won every oil and gas project and much more.

Having won the prestigious Dubai bank job, I had to accommodate two project engineers to manage the project. Chris Rutt was first to come out to the UAE and the most senior, very competent and better still a fisherman. What a breakthrough, every possible weekend it was fishing in various parts of the UAE which I will come to in a later chapter. The 'weakest' point was his love of chicken nuggets and large brandies so our evenings were interesting to say the least. We found him a flat (our agent actually) and chose furniture but he only managed cardboard on all the windows, he never saw the need for curtains. I liked Chris very much, an excellent guy, very well read whose family were all London doctors/consultants. Linda had found a good flat which, compared to Chris's, was upmarket; they also got on well together. The bank project was a real pain but was worth close to a million pounds in order value, even with nearly zero margin however, it was badly needed.

It then became obvious that the company was going to be sold and the two main contenders were Kidde and Tyco. The Kidde offer was higher but with performance strings related to projected profit over two years so I pushed hard for the cash deal from Tyco with no strings attached. Perhaps I had more detailed knowledge of the orders taken at low margins! The board eventually settled on Tyco and all the directors left with buckets of money almost immediately, I was the exception. I also got the cash settlement but was asked to stay with Tyco and move to Qatar to run their oil and gas business. I thought about it for a couple of weeks but did not like the reporting line or people I would report to so they made me redundant, with a nice little pay off. The rest of my staff stayed for a while and gradually were let go or themselves left, Linda took up a key job with a UAE company but eventually the project staff went back to the UK.

I was now out of a job again but got an interview with BAE at Stanmore so delayed the removal company and flew to the UK to hopefully get the job. However, another twist came when I was contacted by Kidde to attend an interview at their HQ in Colnbrook, near Heathrow. Only later did I learn that my name had been put forward by John Robertson, the man from Al Kurdi in Saudi Arabia, who, at that time was managing the Kidde office! 'Onwards and upwards' as my old boss at Astra would say but at last, I was financially secure with no tax liability.

Kidde

I flew to the UK, unemployed yet again, with the intention of trying hard to get the job at BAE systems and returning to work in the UK. It was a good interview and I was told I had the job and the formal offer would be in the post within days – I was delighted. The next morning my eldest daughter, Maria, came in and after a while said, "Why are you so grumpy, Dad?" My response being that I was going for an interview at Kidde and didn't want the job. She said, "Well, don't go," but I told her I had to even if out of politeness though it would probably be over quickly. I drove to Colnbrook and met at 1000 hours with a boss of Detector Electronics, a US subsidiary who manufactured precision detectors primarily for the oil and gas market. He was trying to recruit me as a sales manager only to be told to stop the clock as a much bigger opportunity had arisen and needed discussion!

I should explain that Kidde was a major supplier of high-quality fire protection, detection, suppression and building management products from factories in the US, UK and Europe with further acquisitions planned to expand the product range so an area where I had good background knowledge and personal reputation. This new job opportunity was to manage their Middle East office which was not performing and needed to be sorted out and the business grown significantly.

The interview started with a general chat with a senior director followed by a more detailed discussion with Dr Peter Moore the Technical Director all the while being watched by the HR Director. It was now about 1230 hours and they invited me for lunch in their all-staff lunch room. They said no senior appointments were made without the okay from the CEO Michael Harper and he would have lunch with us. We sat down and in came Michael, who shook my hand, sat down and said, "How are you, John, is it right you're joining us?" After lunch and on our own the HR director said, "Why did you not say you knew the CEO?" I said that I had known him for about ten years from my defence days but did not want to cloud the issue. I was asked to wait and at 1700 hours a contract of employment for two plus two years, based in Dubai, with a good package was put in front of me to sign. I told them that I would take it home, read it carefully and let them know next week. This was fantastic! I accepted and turned BAE down.

My immediate boss would be Peter Moore, who had said to start in two weeks – this would be on the 2nd of January, beginning with a whistle stop tour of all our operations in the UK, the US and Europe which would take three weeks. It was thick snow and bloody cold in the US, not like Dubai in any way but I felt at home! The visit went well, I met all the key people and was introduced to all the products but I could tell that I was being kept at arms-length, causing me serious apprehension!

I returned to Colnbrook for a meeting with Peter and he outlined that I may encounter problems with the Middle East office staff. They were a law unto themselves, taking not much notice of authority and wouldn't like me on principle with the temporary manager, John Robertson, possibly angry that I had been brought in as Regional Director, when he had put my name forward for consideration, he thought it was for a different position.

I flew back to Dubai and went to the office the next day, what shambles; it was like a holiday camp. I got the three sales managers and the secretary together, introduced myself and said we have two months to sort out this place or I will close the office – shock treatment but they thought I was joking. There was no financial control or basic organisation and the secretary was worse than useless. She said that we only had one parking space for the office car park which we share; "Not anymore," I said, "it's mine." That went down like a lead balloon.

It was no wonder that the previous years' order intake was only about four million pounds from the whole region, which included the Middle East, North Africa, Central Asia and a group of countries that were speculative spot opportunities. I started to draw up travel plans and many controls which began to work and we started to look like a working unit. My biggest issue was the secretary who had to go so I sought legal advice and eventually let her go. I called my old PA, Linda, to ask if she was looking for a job, unfortunately not, but she did find me someone. A few days later, I interviewed Lisa Mann, new to Dubai and had been a PA in the UK, took shorthand and was a divorced girl in her early twenties. She was perfect and accepted my offer and worked for me for seven years; she ran the office with a rod of iron, took no crap from anyone and looked after my interests while I was travelling, an absolute diamond.

I was doing a lot of travelling to all the potential markets in the region, to meet existing distributors and potential distributors. I was also going back to all our operating units to understand what they needed to increase order intake. The operating units shared the total cost of the Middle East Office by order intake percentage so I had to justify the costs. I was travelling more than my sales managers; this was a concern they needed to make more focused effort or we would die.

At the end of the first year, the order intake had gone from four to eleven million pounds and we were under my cost budget. Peter said the performance was outstanding and I was not just a gin and tonic merchant as he had originally thought!

My complement of sales managers had now been increased making a team of six, plus Lisa my PA and myself so we were an expensive operation but were delivering good growing business. My travel was still extensive, fishing was good and golf getting better as the weeks passed by.

An annual visit by Michael Harper was always a pressure but he had his finger on the pulse and on every visit insisted on meeting key distributors in the UAE and at least three additional countries, a week of heavy pressure. He was so supportive and said, "Any decision you make I will support, even if I don't agree." What a sign of trust.

I visited the Far East regional office in Singapore on a regular basis and our key operation in Bangkok, Thailand. This was very helpful business-wise and also improved my golf significantly. My ex-deputy Matt Grierson was running the Singapore office and was doing a sterling job but the company strategy of taking product to market had changed from my way and he was not allowed to replicate and follow my example. A tragic error and business suffered as a result.

My team were good and were responding to my leadership and the fact that I backed them 100 percent and got actively involved with their sales efforts, particularly when things were difficult. I am a firm believer that you are only as strong as your team and I chose my staff very carefully and backed them all the way, I consider they were the best available even if at times quite difficult.

I made many visits to Iran over the years and formed an excellent working relationship with Reza Heidari and his company, Tak Lad. However, many products could not be supplied due to government restrictions. Reza and his family remain good friends to this day.

The years rolled by, we met our order intake targets every year and were always under the cost budget. Even the operational units were responding to our success and I could almost walk on water. The fishing was always fun and usually successful and sometimes my golf was good and I got my handicap of twenty-two on the Creek course, quite an achievement. Then a problem; I knew that an MD vacancy for the new Far East office had come up and I put my deputy forward for the position. Against all the odds, but with Michael Harper's backing on my recommendation, my man got the job, which was great, but made my life difficult for a while. However, you must not hold staff back for selfish reasons and it is very satisfying when they come good and he certainly did.

The office we worked from was low key but very low cost so I made no plans to move as customers seldom visited; we went to them or hired a conference room in a hotel.

One of the best things in the early years was Na'ad Al Sheba Golf and Racing Club, which I visited two or three times a week at least; the best steak! They cooked for me what became called, 'John Sellens Specials', not on the club menu; I ate dozens of them over the years, and used the club for incoming visitors as well; so much so they made me an honorary member. On Thursdays, during the racing season, I would always visit as it was an ideal way to meet senior locals in the trainer and owner boxes where I and my friends were always welcome. The Club was an ideal venue to entertain, which I did regularly; excellent food and live music and I was very well-known, so always had wonderful service. Mum and Dad loved it on their two one-month holidays spent in Dubai over the years and my daughter, Tina, visited with her future husband, I think once. Dad loved the fishing best but I will highlight this later. Unfortunately the Dubai Racing Club moved with the times and a new stadium was built, 'Meydan', after which I stopped visiting as it was never the same. A new Rotana hotel was built next to my apartment which offered a great eating place, 'Five Dining', which many called John's Kitchen, as I ate there nearly every night and knew everyone, wonderful themed buffet every night with drinks included in the fixed price, it was perfect.

On the first floor of my apartment block which was a four-floor building was a hospital so I had immediate treatment on hand when needed! I formed a close friendship with Dr Walid Achi, which lasted for about twenty years until I retired. Walid, of Syrian birth, who had qualified in France, was a top surgeon and the senior partner in the hospital; he became a good friend and was also called upon by myself and a number of my friends for medical help and surgical procedures. Yes, a good friend, excellent surgeon and a person I continue to miss having left the region.

We had a major hiccup when the Iraq invasion of Kuwait was imminent and Kidde decided I had to move most staff out of the UAE for safety reasons. None wanted to go but all had to which was a problem for some whose homes back home were rented out. The only one to refuse to leave was my PA Lisa Mann who said she was locally employed (not an expat as such) and if the company insisted, she would quit. I managed to get the company to let her stay with me as skeleton in-country staff. I did have good contingency plans to get out, if necessary, possibly on a dhow to India (like Michael Palin!). The company lost a major suppression project in Qatar with the military which really upset me as the operating company in the UK, Kidde Fire Protection, kept me out of the picture saying they had it covered! Being pig headed, I flew to Doha, met a Sheikh in the Royal family and salvaged the order. Great news and I had formed a key relationship with the Royal family in Doha, which is strong to this day.

Heien Larsson was a UTC Group company in Scandinavia which, in turn, had an operation in Fujairah (an eastern emirate of UAE). The office in Fujairah was managed by a Norwegian, his assistant a young Philippina clerk. The company provided fire protection, technical support to ships anchored in port, however, it also worked, unofficially, as ships' chandler. This operation was not part of my responsibility even though I was regional MD. However, on a call from my CEO reporting that the Norwegian manager had died suddenly of a brain tumour whilst in the shower, I was asked to go and sort things out. I found a rather maverick set up, virtually no records, all business done in cash and a clerk who knew nothing; and kept crying and calling me Sir! Heien Larsson decided the operation should be closed, which was fine in principle but far from easy locally as the manager was dead. I was tasked with doing the closure, which ultimately took about eight months, following local regulations.

The company was registered in the Fujairah Free Zone; had a trading licence, also held stock, had creditors and a bank account. Initially, I had to be made a Heien Larsson director with Power of Attorney then become registered locally. I went to Fujairah frequently for months, arranging disposal of stock and paying creditors; working with local accountants to form company accounts and getting friendly with the local bank and Free Zone director. The closure was completed in late December and having paid off the Philippina clerk, I thought a job well done and Heien Larsson were satisfied. A twist in the tale came however, on Christmas Eve, the Philippina clerk (not now an employee) called me, hysterical and saying come at once Sir, my five-year-old niece is dead in a fire. I telephoned Kidde, of course, everyone was gone for Christmas but fortunately I reached Ron Fleming, a director, who offered to fly out to Dubai immediately if this would help but I asked him just to stay available in case I was locked up as the ex-sponsor of this girl. I contacted the British Embassy and the company lawyers in Dubai, then drove to Fujairah, about fifty miles. On arrival, I found out that the child had been left unattended and a lit Christmas tree had fallen over, starting a fire, the toxic smoke had killed the child. Police and Civil Defence were in attendance and I expected to be arrested with all involved as an offence had been committed and a child was dead. To cut a long story short, no-one was arrested but it was a close-run thing. Over the coming weeks, I had to arrange for the child's body to be flown to Manila with the family; all very upsetting and stressful. I did manage to keep the incident out of the newspapers as it was a tragic accident; remember that we were a company world-leading in fire protection so any press coverage could have been damaging!

I had expanded my staff with more expats and taken the order intake to over hundred million pounds so was still well thought of by the group and reporting to Peter Moore was always a pleasure and the support from Michael Harper exceptional. Then, the not unexpected happened; the group, which now included Chubb Fire, was sold to UTC (United Technologies Corporation) who had decided to move into the fire and security business; my very happy days were part over but I was left alone for a number of years as I kept producing the necessary annual growth at a modest cost. Kidde and Chubb were PLC listed under Williams Holdings, which was a step backwards and the team of so-called experts were not very nice people and sold to UTC, making very good financial gains.

Without doubt, my life in Dubai was a very happy time in all respects, but working for a major American conglomerate was not part of the plan and took its toll with daily conference telephone calls and crazy management requirements and stringent rules; they thought they knew it all but did not. I was to host regular visits to the region by the President and a massive entourage which would last for three or four days with intensive presentations and everything organised down to the smallest detail. These visits took years off my life but were always a success and did me no harm at top level.

Unfortunately my PA, Lisa Mann, moved on, which was a big loss as she had been so good. I had about three more PA's over the coming years and whilst they were okay, they were not in the same class as Lisa, but such is life. Then came another crisis when the latest one quit, I think because I worked her too hard, but Linda was looking for a new challenge and offered her services for a short while on a temporary basis; my prayers had been answered and I had someone who was excellent and I could trust. As I have said before, you are only as strong as your team.

I also lost another of my key men, Nick Barker, who I put forward to run Guardfire, which was based in Thailand; he went as GM but came back to me after a four-year tour which was my lucky day. My other key man was Steve Wilson, another excellent guy who eventually left to join a private company and is currently making his fortune; I must remember to send him a begging letter!

UTC started to become interested in my operation and the first action was to try to change our bonus system from an order intake target to a profit basis; they failed. Next, they wanted all our contracts of employment changed to local contracts; they failed. Next, they wanted to deduct tax at source from our pay; they failed. You could say I was becoming a little unpopular but we were still achieving good business, which helped a lot and surely was the main thing? The next crackpot idea was that they wanted me to fire a number of our product distributors in various countries that were not performing well; not possible without mutual consent, so again failed. Then, in came a high-powered Frenchman, Eric Patry, who had worked for Kidde for some years and wanted to transform the Middle East operation by forming Joint Ventures (JVs) in key countries, primarily using existing Carrier organisations. Eric reported direct to the President, was very rich and powerful, but did not have any experience in the Middle East.

I actually liked Eric, even though I did not always like some of his ideas. The first was to form an agreement with Mr Abdulla, a big player in the UAE and the Carrier distributor for Russia plus a number of other territories. He had grown the Carrier business from nothing to tens of millions over a number of years and was the golden boy in the eyes of UTC. My opinion was that he could not replicate his success with fire products for various reasons, particularly due to the strict approvals required and product pricing levels. I was not believed and I actually signed the UTC agreement on behalf of the President. It never worked, Abdulla invested millions and no significant order growth was achieved, however, I got on well with Abdulla and we are good friends with mutual respect.

During my career in defence, I was unable ever to visit Russia, due to reasons of MOD security. In fact I was not even allowed to route through Moscow when flying east on long haul flights or on my return to the UK. This was particularly difficult when visiting the Far East. However, whilst still bound by the official secrets act, I managed to get permission in the latter years of my career in fire and security whilst at United Technologies Corporation (UTC) to attend an exhibition in Moscow. The exhibition was totally fire-oriented and I travelled from Dubai with one of Mr Abdulla's senior directors for a three-day visit. It was an interesting visit; the exhibition was limited but I had over a day sightseeing in Moscow which was eye opening and I wished it could have been a longer stay. I saw a lot being escorted at all times by one of Mr Abdulla's local managers. I would say I was still tentative being there so did not feel entirely relaxed and safe in the country but it was a great experience which I never thought would happen. I think that the western world does not really understand this extraordinary and massive country or its people and we are perhaps still blinded by the Cold War era, historically anticipated dangers and their various political regimes.

Eric started to target a number of Middle East countries to form JVs via Carrier existing operations which included Egypt, East Africa, Saudi Arabia, Turkey, Oman, Kuwait, Bahrain, Qatar and the UAE. We flew to them all many times, often accompanied by two or three of his team but all proved to be a waste of time and a lot of money. He now started to listen to my ideas at long last, which, after much effort, many more flights and visits, produced formal JVs in Kuwait, Qatar and the UAE before the UTC strategy to Fire and Security changed. Throughout this process and heavy workload, I continued to manage the Middle East office.

I did a number of flights on one of the company jets with Eric and his team to Oman and Saudi Arabia, but the planned JVs did not happen. My staff secured two massive orders during this period, a twelve-million aircraft fire trainer for Dubai and a more than twenty-million for fire trainers for Qatar. This was almost magic and the two single biggest fire orders ever won by the Group and we received many performance awards.

The JV in Qatar was a tough challenge, but with my strong links to the Royal family, and past success rate, enabled a positive result to be achieved. My strong friendship with Ibrahim Al Qaq, a very well-respected local businessman, was a major factor in this success, an honest and clever gentleman with whom I enjoyed working.

However, I believe that UTC were breaking Kidde, Chubb and all the other fire companies they had bought along the way; not experienced enough and this was borne out when they started to sell off the companies. This was mayhem and a tragic result and perhaps typical so I decided to resign and take early retirement from a job I loved, but it was just too much to continue with this management structure and poor judgement. At least I left with last year's orders at over hundred-million and no black marks.

Me and some of my team from Kidde attending race meet

Mum and Dad in Dubai, in their 80s

My good friend Ron Fleming with me at the Dubai Creek Golf and
Racing Club

Abu Dhabi, signing a UTC contract

UTC Fire & Security
A United Technologies Company

February 16, 2009

John,

Congratulations on leading the team that won the 2008 President's Award for Cross Business Unit Collaboration. This award is testimony to your outstanding leadership of the Middle East Office and the spirit of cooperation that you have created across this large and important region.

Well-done John! Keep up the good work — we're still only just getting started in the ME region!

Bill Brown

UTC Corporation Award 2008

Chapter 11
South America

I have already spoken a little about Brazil, but the west coast was where my most regular visits started, initially in Venezuela, promoting Cymbeline with Corris for EMI. The agent we had was a declared and self-confessed Nazi who said he escaped from Germany after the war. We did no business through him and I cannot say I was disappointed; he was a very arrogant man who claimed that the best day of his life was the march into France.

The real interest came with the first Defence Sales expo for UK businesses on an RFA (Royal Fleet Auxiliary) ship which was decked out for exhibition purposes with hardware for demonstration.

The first cruise started in Caracas in Venezuela, then on to Cartagena in Columbia, followed by Sullana in Ecuador and Lima in Peru. This was great and as I flew ahead to each country and waited for the ship to arrive; I had free time to enjoy some sightseeing at the company's expense, not a normal occurrence.

Firing demonstrations were provided in each country, which entailed taking all the hardware to an artillery range, initially for practice then for a full-blown firing demonstration. This included artillery, tanks, vehicles, radars and much more and many sales were subsequently achieved from these demonstrations.

Columbia was an interesting visit, into the port of Cartagena and the firing ranges about seventy miles away. Again, I spent all my time supporting our equipment, Cymbeline, as I was acting as the support engineer; this was very demanding work. Cartagena is an interesting city and the Fort, incredible. It was built to hold and protect all the South American gold but failed when Drake came calling and pinched the lot; we are not popular as they have long memories.

On my first visit to Cartagena, I stayed at the Don Blas hotel, which was a standard high-rise hotel, opening onto the wonderful beach. My good friend, Les Knight from MEL, tried to teach me to swim off this beach and after drinking what seemed like gallons of sea water, he admitted that I really could not swim. Les spoke Spanish and dealt with all MEL defence business into South America and Spain. We did have a great friendship that lasted until he passed away in 2019. On my next trip into Cartagena, I went upmarket and stayed at the big old fashioned Hotel Cartagena that featured in the film 'Romancing the Stone'.

In Ecuador, we drove to Sullana, the most westerly point on the coast and a centre for Marlin fishing (too expensive for me to try out). The firing ranges were about fifty-miles away, so again, much driving in convoy and as always, very demanding. On the demonstration day, a local General asked me for the approximate cost of a Cymbeline Mortar Locating Radar; I reluctantly told him and he shook his head, saying, "For that amount of money, I can bribe the enemy to stop fighting." This was when I wondered what I was doing in sales!

The army sales team and a handful of company representatives all stayed at the only hotel in Sullana. In fact, I think that we were the only guests. The senior British officer sent his only dress uniform for cleaning but it took three days to come back, during which time he was confined to the hotel! At the end of the visit, everyone left except my good friend, Andy, and I. Then to pay the bill; no way could we pay, credit cards were unacceptable, likewise sterling travellers' cheques and we were short of ready cash. The hotel insisted I stay as a guarantee but allowed Andy to travel to Guayaquil, which was a trip of about ninety-miles each way to cash travellers' cheques at a local bank. He went by bus with chickens and goats, which took a full day; what a performance! The moral of the story, always carry cash when in South America and make sure it's US dollars.

The visit to Lima, in Peru, was very interesting but not, in my opinion, likely to produce sales, but you can never be sure what might happen and if you don't try you never are likely to succeed.

The Defence Sales initiatives were repeated in each territory of South America in the same way as further RFA tours to Africa, the Middle East, Europe and the Far East, every one of which, fortunately for me, I was present to support. The RFAs used were Tarbatness, Lyness, Sir Lancelot and Stromness. All great ships doing a wonderful job; the parties were great too and food fantastic. It must have cost a fortune but the costs were shared with the UK companies involved. What a wonderful way to demonstrate the might and quality of British military export products to friendly countries.

Brazil in the east of the South American Continent is a beautiful and fascinating country but so dangerous, where life is cheap and killing and theft the norm. I have detailed some experiences in this wonderful country in earlier chapters but it really does deserve more. The Copa Cabana beach has to be seen to be believed and I was fortunate to stay at Le Meridian hotel, right at the end of the beach, many times. The problem was, as you left the hotel for the beach, hotel security would ensure that you were in your swimwear and advice was to carry only a towel or you would be robbed. Jewellery, camera, watch, anything of value made you a prime target – I witnessed a robber shot dead with a fisherman's spear gun only thirty yards from me whilst he was running up the beach, having robbed someone else of their watch! Without doubt, this country would be my top tourist destination but for the violence. My good friend, Les Knight, from the MEL Company, showed me many of the sights and his knowledge of Spanish was invaluable when ordering drinks and fantastic big steaks. I also travelled north into the interior, tracing the Amazon to Manaus, right in the heart of the jungle; a very special experience.

My one and only visit to Bolivia started at arrival at La Paz airport. The airport, El Alto, is actually about eight miles from La Paz city, and is at 4,062 m (13,327 feet) above sea level, which is the highest international airport in the world. The planes descend very slowly when landing and seem to struggle when taking off. However, the hard bit is to deplane without collapsing due to the altitude, not a place to move quickly or carry bags, even a briefcase is a struggle. Altitude sickness and other side effects can be almost instant on arrival and many passengers need oxygen immediately! I would not have Bolivia on my holiday list but it is an intriguing country with wonderful places to see and visit.

South America is a wonderful region but dangerous. However, I got to know a number of Kidde people who were on the tours there which was to come in handy a few years later. I also had some very memorable times and made some good friends, furthermore I had my long-term friend, Andy Anderson, from EMI, with me for much of the time which was another bonus.

My good friend Andy, in Peru.
"Do you like my hat, John?"

Chapter 12
Africa

My first travels to Africa were in the early seventies, to South Africa, when defence business was allowed. A wonderful country in those days but has, in my opinion, gone downhill steadily since majority rule was introduced but I guess 'that's progress'.

My work in the early days was with Barlow Rand and ARMSCOR and was very interesting and rewarding. I also met some great people, who have remained friends over the years. EMI had a record company there and the General Manager was a guy called Dudley Lewis. I only met him once and he was not involved with the Defence business but said to me, a visit to the Kruger Park for a long weekend was a must and arranged it at company expense; what a gentleman. The visit was fantastic; we flew in an old DC3, slept in a Rondavel (round thatched hut), and spent three days meeting the animals. To put it in perspective, the park is the size of Wales and the silence is unbelievable.

I did many visits to South Africa but the early ones were the best, staying in The Burgers Park Hotel in Pretoria. The BA flight in those days had to stop in Nairobi to refuel, which was often a problem because due to the airport altitude and temperature, the flight was often delayed.

The other main destinations on my visits to the African Continent were to Kenya, Tanzania, Zanzibar, Uganda, Zimbabwe, Botswana, Angola, Ethiopia, Sudan, Ghana, Nigeria, Zambia, Burkina Faso, Congo, Namibia, Egypt, Libya, Tunisia, Algeria, Morocco and Mauritania. This is a wonderful Continent and I can honestly say I had some fantastic visits and was always treated well and with respect and kindness, with perhaps one exception.

In earlier chapters, I have touched on some of the visits to African countries but for the full detail it would take too much space and perhaps become a bit boring; I am therefore just highlighting some key events and experiences. For example, I flew from Casablanca down to Laayoune, close to the border with Mauritania, trying to sell large calibre ammunition. The first problem was when the plane landed, I got off into the desert and eventually realised this was not the expected destination, it was actually a place called Tan Tan! I banged on the now closed aircraft door and was let back in – much to the flight crew's amusement – they had only landed to deliver the mail!

On another visit, this time to Tanzania, I made a trip over to Zanzibar to meet a Minister. I went on a ferry, which was an experience in itself, but on arrival, found no immigration, so I walked on out of the docks and off to my meeting. When I returned after a few hours, I was arrested as I had no inward stamp in my passport, so was not officially in the country. After a lot of talking and some 'payment', an in-and-out stamp appeared in my passport and I was allowed to leave.

The ferry had gone so I flew out on a single-engine private plane for fifty pounds.

On a sales trip to Entebbe in Uganda, I spent four days in a hotel where my room still had dried blood up the walls where Idi Amin's gangsters tortured residents. Not a nice reminder of the atrocities committed during Amin's rule and the Israeli crashed plane was also a reminder of the rescue raid as it was still just off the runway. I was really keen to leave but the first plane out to Nairobi was in three days! It was suggested I take an immediate flight with DHL for fifty pounds, did this mean I was to fly as a parcel? Not quite; but a bloody small twin-engined plane turned up and I took the one seat next to the pilot; off we flew, tree-hopping with the animals, but I lived, and left Uganda never to return.

My visits to Nairobi were many; both when I was in the defence business and fire and security. I usually stayed at the Intercontinental Hotel which almost became a second home whilst I worked for Hall and Watts. However, business was slow, unless overseas aid was available. In later years, the fire protection business was good primarily via my Egyptian agent, Henor, owned and run by Hesham and Nabil Fouad, who had a thriving operation in Kenya via their US based company and managed to get paid. I miss meeting up with Hesham and Nabil on a regular basis; they are good friends with lovely families. I even fully investigated a Joint Venture opportunity with Henor, for UTC, but unfortunately this failed at the eleventh hour. The island of Mombasa was a regular destination for me as this was the home of the Kenyan Navy. A very dodgy chain ferry operated from the mainland but a great place, once across! Mombasa itself was a very interesting place with beautiful beach hotels, white sands, blue sea and plenty of violence.

Nairobi has perhaps a unique restaurant on the outskirts of the city called 'Carnivore'. It serves game meat and as much as you want, cooked on a BBQ in front of you. Everything was served, from crocodile to zebra (no stripes through the meat, by the way). A great place for meat eaters and a really famous place, I loved it.

It was a privilege to visit Botswana and whilst I never won any business, it was a fantastic country; nice people, and if you like the bush and wildlife, put it on your holiday list. It used to be run by the Khama twins who were good friends of my friend and mentor Stephen Kock, so I am surprised no business was won. Hall and Watts Middle East had an office there, run by a Brit, which was quite successful for a period of time but I was excluded from any involvement! I could have helped.

When I visited Harare, I was lucky to be given a personal contact to the sister of a senior member of my masonic lodge, Geoffrey Pinder. His sister, Beryl was married to Jack, a great guy and super couple who ran a farm and managed a gold mine at a place called 'Acturus', about a one-hour drive from Harare. I stayed with them many times and their hospitality was fantastic, even during difficult times. Jack took me down the gold mine, which was a hell of an experience, and we also played golf at the police club in Harare a number of times and met many of his friends. This golf course was very tiring as the club is at about 5,000 feet above sea level. Wonderful times and both Jack and Beryl were so kind to me and Jack's stories about the war very colourful, but for certain, very true. It's a tragedy this country was wrecked and plundered by the

President and his henchmen over decades, the local people suffered so much and still are, due to corruption and, I believe, the loss of the white minority, particularly the farmers. The threat, particularly if you were white, of the Chikurubi jail, which has a notorious reputation for brutality, torture, mistreatment of prisoners and human rights abuses was ever present.

On a visit to Kenya, I flew from Lagos in Nigeria, from west to east, which is not ideal on Ethiopian airways and the plane had a technical issue when it landed in Addis Ababa. Big problem and I was stuck there in a hotel for three days with my passport held at the airport as I had no visa. With a grim hotel, even grimmer food, no beer and not allowed out of the hotel, all in all a difficult journey. I knew I should have flown north from Lagos to London and then back south to Nairobi, but hindsight is a wonderful thing.

I consider Egypt to be part of the Middle East for business purposes, but it is actually part of the African Continent, hence I am writing about it in this chapter. Making many visits over the years, it is hot, busy and dusty; vastly different from city to city. It has wonderful places to see and explore and very interesting people. Such a deep, fascinating history, of course, and the Egyptians having provided so much towards the modern way of life; their engineers were well known for their expertise and in our times are involved with so many major construction projects in the Middle East region. The problem is corruption and they joke that if you shake hands with an Egyptian, check to see if you still have all your fingers! I made many friends there, however, and they were honest and straight, which helped me a lot and I supplied a significant amount of fire safety products over the years. A close British friend lost a relative during the last war, who died of his wounds in Alexandria, and was buried in one of the cemeteries; after an investigation, the grave was found for me by my good friend from Henor, retired Colonel Nabil Fouad, who so kindly sent us photographs of the grave and surrounds. Colonel Nabil Fouad is a war hero from the '67 war with Israel and I often spent evenings with him and his air force friends over the years and we all drank a lot of whisky together and I heard so many stories of true valour, so, so interesting.

In recent years I always stayed at the Marriott Hotel, not far from Cairo International Airport, very lush and with a beautiful 18-hole golf course which I have played many times. The hotel has many other sports facilities. Cairo airport covers a vast area and is heavily defended as are all major facilities in the country – they stand ready for war and are militarily very strong.

Morocco was also a regularly visited country whilst I was working for Hall and Watts Middle East, primarily for the potential supply of artillery ammunition. Not a place that I liked very much and which I found boring, even though I travelled throughout the country which is vast; however, it deserves its place whilst talking about north Africa as it is a major player in the area.

Accra, in Ghana, was interesting to visit, the people were nice and the beer was good. On my first visit, my agent met me at the airport, picked up my bag and put it on his head. I said to him that surely he would hurt his head, but his reply came back saying, "No, but it would hurt my arms if I carried it!" My hotel, I use the word loosely, was at the local horse-riding stables just a room, no facilities and very smelly. The business here was low value and funds found from UN expenses for Ghana serving military personnel!

On another visit to Accra, in Ghana, I went to a hotel to check in and in the reception lobby was a beautiful Dalmatian dog. I asked the receptionist if the dog was friendly, "Yes," she said, so I stepped forward only to have a lump bitten out of the top of my leg! It then left me to try to savage a Japanese businessman, who had followed me into the hotel. Five days later, I flew back to the UK and went to see my GP, who said rabies was a possibility and called World Health; oh my goodness. I fortunately only had the first two of a horrendous course of injections (two in the bum but the next would have been in the stomach whilst in hospital). The reason for the halt in treatment was my agent in Accra was able to confirm that the dog was still alive after two weeks, meaning it did not have rabies. Happy days!

No successful businessman involved with exports from the UK into Africa can have failed to visit Nigeria. This country is a major trading partner with the UK, has enormous oil wealth and its vast population is in poverty. It is dirty, very corrupt and extremely dangerous for every nationality including the local population. There is no trust and everyone at all levels seems to be on the take, the only difference is the level of corruption. I visited many times and did some very significant defence and commercial business, none of which was enjoyable or satisfying and I am glad to say I will never need to go back.

I give some examples of some of the everyday things that happened which may be hard to believe if you have never visited. Having arrived and managed to get out of the airport unscathed, not easy, then reached the hotel, where you have a confirmed booking, the problems really start: no booking? But you have it confirmed in writing but without more money changing hands, no room.

When you reach the room, you do not settle in until you are sure it is empty, look in the wardrobe, behind the shower curtain then once in, lock the door. I carried a special internal security lock to ensure no one could enter. This is real. Attacks, muggings, theft and hostage taking are normal activity.

Taxis are very dangerous and you can be threatened or taken hostage at any time. Money is the only thing that works, if you are lucky. Leaving should be a happy experience but it is not, payment at every stage is required and do not be surprised when on the plane if a number of people have the same boarding card seat number!

I could say so much more but I think enough is enough and it is such a shame such a rich country can be so awful, not for me ever again at any price.

Chapter 13
The Far East

The majority of the Far Eastern countries are very welcoming to visitors and apart from the weather and bugs; it is a wonderful place to visit on business or pleasure.

I have spent a tremendous amount of time over the years in this region and have visited most of the countries. It has always been interesting and enjoyable and generally the people are friendly and pleased to entertain visitors. My initial visits to the region were via RAF flights before I had the luxury of commercial airlines. The RAF flights normally started at Lyneham or Brize Norton and, if lucky, were on a VC10, not a C130. The seats faced the back of the plane for safety and the packed lunch and no alcohol, all part of the in-flight service. The next major issue was flight time, amazing when compared with today. The initial leg arrived in Akrotiri in Cyprus with a night stop, then to Masirah Island in Oman, with a night stop, then to Gan in the Maldives and a night stop, then Singapore and a rest unless flying on to Australia. What an ordeal and the RAF night stop accommodation was basic, to say the least. No mobile phones or communications during days of travel, thank goodness when I flew BA and even better when the Jumbo 747s came into service.

Sri Lanka is an interesting place. The tsunami which struck was so very devastating. As it happened, the CEO of Kidde was on a visit there with some of his family over that Christmas period. His son was on the Harrow cricket tour and playing cricket in Galle when the tsunami hit, they were all very lucky to survive. I was called upon to visit the area to see what Kidde, as a company could do, to help in this disaster; it really was a tragic sight to see. It took about ten hours to drive from Colombo to Galle as all the bridges were out. I saw the train still on its side where over 1000 people died and many bodies were still hanging in the trees; it was a horrendous sight. I also went further south to Matara, where the devastation was terrible and after my initial assessment, I returned to Dubai to decide what we might do to help. Giving money was not my preferred option due to potential corruption. My suggestion was to help set up a fire and rescue station in Matara as there was nothing like this currently in place. What a task, but with the help of a Sri Lankan Minister, land was allocated; an Italian company supplied vehicles and a building and we at Kidde supplied all the fire-fighting equipment. I also managed to get the fire chief in Colombo, Mr Knangera, a personal friend, to provide men and training. The task came together well and we all hope that the residents of Matara benefit from everyone's efforts after such a destructive and tragic event which affected so many lovely people.

Thailand is perhaps my favourite country in the Far East region and I always found the people to be friendly. It is also a low-cost destination in business or for holidays, their beach resorts are so beautiful. I must have visited at least thirty or forty times on defence business and was able to stay at the better hotels as well as play golf at many of their fantastic courses. My last family holiday there, which included my mum and dad, was for three weeks over a Christmas and New Year period; it was a great holiday but my mum missed her turkey lunch on Christmas day, she had to make do with delicious sea food! I usually stayed at The Oriental Hotel in Bangkok during my many visits and this was and may still be one of the best hotels in the world, I would judge it in the top ten for sure. On one occasion, I had to meet with the boss of the coast guard regarding a requirement for medium calibre ammunition; he came by boat and moored up at the Oriental Hotel with his entourage and we met in a private bar! Quite a wonderful change for business negotiations and we made a sale. Admiral, Sir Derek Empson, also used The Oriental on occasions when he had to support the business on a number of my visits and then we really were given VIP status.

During my many visits to Thailand, I worked with assistance from various organisations one of which was G H International owned and operated by Sarabjit Singh. Sarabjit ran a highly professional, family business, strong in various market sectors. Over the years I got to know the family well as I worked with his company on a number of projects. The fantastic hospitality extended to me and my family in both business and pleasure continues to be appreciated and I would welcome the opportunity to meet up again.

Malaysia is yet another gem of the Far East and is another place that features high on my visit list; I made many friends at varying levels, from the PM downwards. It is linked by road to Singapore but very different in so many ways, my business visits there were all related to defence sales as fire and security issues were dealt with from the Singapore and Thai offices. Kuala Lumpur (KL) is a very interesting and welcoming place and I did the train journey from Singapore on a number of occasions, which was always a test of stamina. A very famous railway link from our colonial past! You just need to keep drinking lots of gin and tonic (the quinine helps to kill the malaria from the mosquitoes and the gin keeps you happy). I had many good friends in KL, who I often met in the casinos in London (Palm Beach, Sporting Club, The Hilton, Crockfords and The Clarmont Club) when they visited, as the top boys love to gamble and most are members of the key Mayfair clubs. I never gambled and only watched, sometimes they lost many thousands but never seemed to be upset, another plus for being in the defence business. On one particular contract negotiation, which after signing, the senior officer said he needed a favour for his wife; my first thought was a new car! In fact, he said his wife had a 1950s Morris Minor, her pride and joy but the windscreen seal leaked and let in rain, could I help? I got a replacement seal from a friend in New Zealand and it arrived by DHL courier within days, problem solved and friends for life and lots more business.

My visits to Manila in the Philippines and Jakarta in Indonesia were always eventful and challenging, especially Brunei, Taiwan, China, South Korea and Japan; however all were very interesting and always an experience. Again, these visits were primarily defence-related and many orders were secured.

Hong Kong was also a regular destination as it was a key travel hub and always novel to land and take off from the old airport. To fly in was frightening as the high-rise towers were so close to the runway, so much so that in the evening, you could look into the rooms and see the inhabitants very clearly because the aircraft was lower than the top of the buildings! It really was one of the wonders of the world and must have been a real tester for a pilot's nerve and skill – the runway was also quite short so no room for error. In later years, the new airport was built and fortunately, Thorn Security supplied all the fire protection products, which was a massive order for us.

I have talked about Singapore earlier but in many ways, it was a home from home for me. It does present as a rather clinical place particularly in recent years after so much of the old town was destroyed to make way for the 'new Singapore' – guess this is progress once again. It was perhaps never the same after the British Military left, which I consider to be a tragic political decision, and cost us to lose a massive amount of trade into the region (even now you can get a suit made in a day in Singapore and it will fit perfectly). Over the years in Singapore, it was a pleasure to be associated with Jardine Matheson, a major facilitator, working together with Joseph Chia, senior executive. Joseph and his wife, Maria, have remained good friends to this day and even managed a visit to my home whilst on holiday in the U.K. with their young sons.

I visited China in 1980, with a team from EMI, to present Cymbeline and we took a lot of hardware with us. The visit took about seven weeks and we did come away with a contract. I believe the first for a military product from the UK and the western world. It was tough working there seven days a week but an excellent experience, the food was grim and hotel 'basic', costing 3.5 pounds a week, yes; a week, for bed, breakfast and laundry. What you do to achieve a sale but The Friendship Hotel in Beijing was the best and the only international hotel there at the time!

I could write so much about this region as it is generally a wonderful place but perhaps the '70s and '80s were by far the best years for me.

A moment of R&R whilst at the RAF Station, Gan, Maldives

Chapter 14
The Lebanon

Without doubt, Lebanon is a beautiful country and was well known as the ideal holiday destination on the Mediterranean back in the sixties and early seventies. It was also the banking hub for the region in those days, which then moved to Dubai. This all changed because of the devastating war which started in the early seventies and lasted decades with many people killed and property bombed, which then became derelict. I was fortunate to visit before the war but then visited many times once the war finished and the rebuilding commenced.

My visits initially were related to defence opportunities, but soon were focused on fire and security matters. This was related to Thorn Security, Kidde and UTC with product supply via a number of local distributors which had support organisations.

I got to know many of the distributors quite well, particularly Beydoun Fire and Security, which is owned by Mohamed Beydoun, a charming ex-Minister, whose family is very well known in Lebanon, a nicer and more honest family it would be hard to meet. Over the years, Mohamed, his daughter Nina, and son Yussef, became very close friends. We met in Beirut, Dubai, Turkey, the USA and other places when fire product training was being done or contracts discussed so we had very close links.

My CEO at Kidde (Michael Harper), visited on one occasion and I arranged for him to meet Mohamed Beydoun. Michael said, "Is he important and where are we meeting?" When I said, "In the Prime Minister's Office."

He replied, "Yes, this is a VIP!" We had an excellent meeting followed by drinks.

On one occasion, I flew into Beirut on a Sunday morning from Dubai, expecting to start work the following day. As I came down the steps of the plane, there, on the tarmac, was Mohamed with his car and two body guards waiting for me, what a good job I had worn a suit! Mohamed led me to the back of the car and asked me what I was doing today. When I told him that I would only be preparing for tomorrow, he said, "You are coming with me then." And opened the boot of the Mercedes, which was full of weapons, he said, "I know you know how to use them if we have problems so, off we go." I asked about immigration but apparently this had been sorted and what a good job I had brought only a carry-on overnight bag with me.

The car, with the two body guards in the front, bristling with weapons set off at breakneck speed, with the siren blaring. I asked where we were going and Mohamed told me we were heading to an old church in Sidon and to my further questions told me there was a Roman Catholic Mass being held to give thanks to UN personnel killed in a helicopter crash in the Bekaa Valley and I was to give condolences on behalf of the UK Government – oh my goodness. He then said I would be in the front pew, sitting with the President, Mr Hariri, so not to worry, I said, "I am not a Catholic." He said,

"No worries," sounding Australian! The church was very old, full of many Ministers and the relatives of the dead and many UN officials, plus one Brit at the back of the church. What an opportunity for a bomb attack! Sure enough, I sat in the front pew with the President, just the two of us, with Mohamed sitting behind me. After the Mass, I lined up and gave condolences to the grieving families, what an ordeal! On my way out, the other Brit came up to me and said, "Who are you?"

I said, "John." And he asked for a business card, which I declined to provide. I said to counter his approach, "Who are you?" He said, "The British Ambassador." Oh my goodness. I was on the TV that night and on the front page of the local paper the next day, what a way to keep low profile!

On the very dangerous drive back to Beirut, at high speed, Mohamed said he would take me to a very special place for dinner, called Fookrar Dean, adding that I would not know anyone and there would be a lot of senior military and plenty of armed security. The place was as he predicted and up in the mountains but, as we walked in, a General in uniform came up, put his arms around me, kissed me and said, "Hello Mr John, come and meet my family and join us for dinner." Mohamed was shocked, saying, "Do you know who this is?" I said, "Yes, he is head of your special forces." Mohamed just looked on and said, "You know some very heavyweight and dangerous people."

I did many visits to Beirut often staying at Nina Beydoun's Hotel 'The Bayview' next door to the Hard Rock Cafe. I always had an armed guard outside my room door twenty-four hours a day; was I a target, I will never know? At this time, Beirut was a very dangerous place to be and occupied by thousands of Syrian troops. One of my staff, not based in Dubai, got into big problems, which caused me to fly out at a moment's notice from Dubai to fix the problem and get him out of country fast, all part of being an MD but thank goodness for special contacts.

On another visit for a few days I ended up in Mohamed's office at about 1100 hours, had coffee, and as I had finished work, expected to return to the hotel, not so. Mohamed picked up the phone, summoned his driver and body guards and said, "Take Mr John to see Baalbek." This was the archaeological site way down south. What a journey of about a hundred miles at breakneck speed, siren wailing and the massive site closed for security. It was opened for me and one guide and my two body guards! This was a highly dangerous visit due to terrorist activity in the area.

Unfortunately, the Lebanon is still a haven for terrorism and military unrest, tragic for such a beautiful place but with no stability in sight.

Chapter 15
The Sultanate of Oman

As the first Middle East country I visited, it is not surprising that it has a very special place in my heart. The people are so nice and it really is a beautiful place with extreme heat, wonderful mountains and then the differing tropical temperatures and vegetation around Salalah in the south.

The country is vast, covering about 300,000 Sq km, with more than 1,700 km of coastline, and is very sparsely populated, about 3.5 million people, the majority being Indian expats. The country includes the Musandam peninsula, which looks over the strategic Straits of Hormuz and is separated from the main country by the UAE. The country also has many islands, the largest being Masirah, which was gifted to the British as an RAF station and is now also used by the American Air Force as well as SOAF, the Omani Air Force. The country has vast desert areas, salt flats, mountains and very fertile farms. The main cities are the capital, Muscat, Sohar to the west and Salalah in the south. A very different climate from the north, Salalah with its green fields, cattle, banana plants, mango and coconut trees, is a tropical environment. During the harif in July/August, the place is shrouded in cloud and rain and the sea is very rough, with high waves hitting the beaches. Driving south from Muscat, you come to Thumrait, which is at about 5,000 feet and you drive down the mountain range into Salalah at sea level. A wonderful drive unless it is in August, when visibility is down to a few yards due to the mist.

The main revenue is from onshore oil and the wells are all located on the eastern part of the country. Oman is still very closely linked to the UK, where we still have considerable influence, particularly the military links where British personnel are deployed on a regular basis and equipment is stock piled. The Omani forces are very well equipped with the latest weaponry and even more importantly are well trained by the British. Strategically, this country is very important in the region.

I first visited in the early seventies, during the war with south Yemen to deliver mortar locating radars from EMI. This resulted in many further visits in the seventies, most of the time being based in the air field officers mess in Salalah. With no hotels at that time, my 'home' (Bayt) was a single room shed with noisy air-conditioning and only saline water. The building was surrounded by oil barrels full of sand stacked up to roof level for shell, bullet, shrapnel protection and a deep trench outside for further protection against the dangers. All good fun looking back, but quite scary at the time and many people were killed. The war with Yemen took many lives over a number of years and the Omani side was run by the British under direction of Sultan Qaboos, the ruler. This country was, and is, a key training area for our military and Special Forces.

I negotiated a number of defence contracts sales during my time at Unwin's and Astra, meeting many of my contacts and the Omani Prime Minister via a mutual Russian friend. I made numerous visits to this wonderful place where I usually stayed at the Intercontinental beach hotel, built in the early seventies and latterly at the Al Bustan (the best hotel in the world in my opinion). Once I moved to live in Dubai, my very regular visits were predominantly by road, initially this journey took about four hours but once the speed cameras were installed, about every two km the journey time increased to five hours. The border post at Hatta Fort was the best crossing point and I went at least once a month for many years, often taking friends or family with me. Buraimi Oasis was another crossing point but not a good option, although I used it a few times.

At Hatta, near the UAE and Oman border, the oasis has been developed into a resort with a small and quirky hotel built to suit its rocky mountainous environment. The pools always made an interesting, cooling walk through, most being ankle deep with lots of frogs to see, but walking further into the mountains, the pools were deep enough for swimming. Hatta itself was a good day out escape from Dubai city and it developed further over the years and after they had made it an administrative border post, with many more small business shops and a museum. Mum and Dad visited a couple of times and loved Oman and were well looked after at the Intercontinental Hotel as I knew the British manager well and he helped a lot. It was a pleasure to see them having such a good time so late in life. They enjoyed Muscat and Ruwi, the countryside, mountains and town markets. The city market in Muscat is fascinating, with its narrow passageways lined by open fronted shops with perfumes, spices, textiles, gemstones and silver; the Omani silver being their particular art is crafted into some very beautiful jewellery and practical items.

Al Sawadi beach was a great place to stay, about seventy miles short of Muscat when driving from Dubai. A hotel development that had recently opened and we discovered after winning a fire, security and building management project at the Sohar Beach hotel, a little to the south. The coastline at Al Sawadi was stunning and walking out at low tide to a nearby island was a magnificent experience, the low tide making it possible to see unusual corals and seabed creatures at close quarters. This was a one-off experience for me (I am no diver), I stayed there many times.

In early January 2020, it was announced that Sultan Qaboos had passed away, aged seventy-nine, and with no heir, so his cousin, Tariq Al Said, was sworn in. This makes him PM, Commander of the Armed Forces, Minister of Defence, Minister of Finance and Minister of Foreign Affairs. This may well cause a power struggle in the coming months and also an issue in the region as Oman is so strategic geographically and within the GCC (Gulf Co-operation Council). Historically, Sultan Qaboos took over from his father in a British led coup in 1970 and over the years, with British help, led the country to prosperity and stability; he was much loved by his people, a great leader and ruler.

The Musandam peninsula, which is right up in the north of Oman, is a beautiful drive up the coast from the border post and views of sea, mountains, and interesting small and isolated villages on the way up to the Golden Tulip hotel to stay as a base. Moving onwards, lays the town of Khasab, with its coastline like the fjords of Norway, interesting quay, museum and small shops. From here, the day trip on an old dhow was my favourite with wonderful sights of other islands, the clear blue water and the dolphins often following alongside the boat, jumping fish and sea birds ducking and diving. A wonderful weekend trip when possible and a positive change from the business of Dubai.

I took some friends on this visit for a day trip from Ras Al Khaimah, where they were staying. It was exceedingly hot and I had just returned from the UK, having had knee surgery, so a long drive and being on a dhow for the day was not maybe ideal. On the way back to RAK, about half way, we stopped to have a stretch on a beach at about 1700 hours, just getting dark and still with a temperature in the forties. Somehow, my car keys ended up in the sea, retrieved but not working, what to do? Fortunately, some Omanis stopped and kindly took me to the border where I formally re-entered the UAE with much walking to phone Avis in Dubai, who, two hours later, brought a spare key. Then to cross the border again, get a lift back to my car and continue the journey, getting my friends to their hotel in RAK at about midnight, what an adventure we did not need!

In the very early days of visits to Oman, I spent much time staying with Air Work Services in Seeb, which is at the site of the international airport. They had a large staff, many from the British Services and most were located at Seeb but they also had staff throughout the Sultanate. They looked after me well and I made many friends. I then progressed to various major Omani companies, one of which was Electroman, who were the top distributor for Thorn Security and installed fire detection and suppression products in all the prestigious buildings. They were also big in defence, either direct or via one of the subsidiary companies. The group was owned by the Prime Minister, who was also Minister of Defence, so all military purchases went through one of his companies, no surprise. I visited the palace to meet the Minister, who was top royal family, also meeting his wives and some of his children; his last wife being British (a tough lady). It was sad when he passed away of prostate cancer, his number one son was fourth in line for the throne.

I established contacts in many Omani companies over the years and was quite high profile in many market sectors. On a visit with the UTC President and his entourage on the private jet we went for a VIP dinner with a top old Omani businessman who, by the main course at a circular table with about twenty guests, looked at me and said, "I know you." I said, "You do sir, it was in the early seventies during the war."

"Oh yes," he said, "I remember, do you remember that gentleman on your left, he is now the Chief of the air force (SOAF)?" We continued to talk and the UTC President was a little ignored.

I made two nostalgic visits to Salalah after 1990, once by car, staying at the Palm Beach Hotel, which was then a tired Crowne Plaza and once by air and then stayed at the newly opened Hilton. The initial visit was during the harif, so it was misty or raining most of the time but so interesting and caused me to be moved to considerable emotion at times. I actually met the editor of the local newspaper in the bar at the hotel who claimed that all the locals owed their lives to the British military, of which I was one. He wanted my story, but as always, I turned the press down, perhaps I was wrong! I visited Mirbat, where the famous SAS battle took place and Taqa and Raysut, all places I remember so well. I did some fishing in the heavy surf and actually caught fish, which the hotel cooked for dinner. The second visit staying at the Hilton was very different but very enjoyable.

I could say so much more about Oman but suffice it to say a wonderful, wonderful place and very hospitable people, perhaps, for me, the best in the Arab world.

Oman, 1973

Cymbeline equipment, Salalah, Oman

My 'home' on Palm
Beach,
Salalah, Oman.

The Living Room.
The protective barrels.
Me, ready for anything.

Chapter 16
The Gulf Cooperation
Council (GCC)

The GCC was founded on May 25th 1981, the founding countries being: the United Arab Emirates, Saudi Arabia, Qatar, Oman, Bahrain and Kuwait. With its headquarters in Riyadh, it included all the Arab states, with the exception of Iraq. Ras Al Khaimah joined the GCC in 1982.

My business travels and some holidays took me to all the GCC states many times over the years and I have mentioned some of my experiences earlier in the book and in various chapters. I made many local and expat friends and I have considerable respect for the development and progress made by the local communities against significant odds but oil wealth has helped significantly.

Whilst they are all Muslim, the culture and customs still vary considerably country by country. All are very tribal and defence prepared, particularly in Oman, whose history is based on trade and where and when necessary military activity. For my part, I tried to be totally neutral of local customs, religion and political activity. This was particularly hard for me due to my activities in Oman in the early 70s and my love of that country and the people.

I believe that the British still hold a special place in the hearts of the individual Arab countries' Rulers and GCC in general, although the USA and latterly the Chinese have somewhat eroded this 'special' relationship. The GCC was formed to boost trade and economic growth and ideally to diversify from the reliance on oil production, this has been most successfully achieved by Dubai. Security and military coordination in defence was also a key in the group relationship, however tribal and religious differences have proved difficult to resolve internally.

Saudi Arabia is a vast territory, predominantly desert, with huge onshore oil reserves and now a massive petrochemical industry. The first oil well became productive in the early 1930s in the Eastern Province. It is a restrictive society, particularly for foreigners, but for locals as well, where Sharia law is strictly applied and obeyed. An expat must observe local customs and laws, failing to do so can be very harshly enforced with draconian and sometimes medieval penalties. This is a country where you never quite feel at ease, as a visitor you have no rights. Women must be properly dressed in an abaya with head covered and accompanied by husband or male family member when out of the house. It is only recently that women have been allowed, in some areas, to drive cars, though few do so. The prayer times must be strictly observed and take place five times a day, where necessary they are enforced by the Mattawa (religious police). Hotels and restaurants have separate eating areas for women, men, families.

I must say that having painted this strict picture, in my numerous visits and having lived in Riyadh for two years, I had no problems. Business can be very lucrative but corruption is rife and local 'agents' can require double figure percentages if orders are to be achieved. Experience and good advice are essential to secure business as is understanding who is key in any deal. This is difficult due to strong family ties and knowing who's who is like working out a puzzle. It is a highly personally challenging country in which to live as an expat or to conduct business.

Qatar is a small country with massive wealth from oil and gas. The capital, Doha, is the heart of this geographically small territory, with a very small local population and their leading ruling family, the Al Thani's. Political and religious issues have caused many issues over the years, particularly recently, when Qatar became isolated from most of the GCC. The country has a strong military, although relatively small and is the home of the US Command Centre which came to the fore during the Gulf war with Iraq. Its links with Saudi Arabia for a number of years have been strained and the land and air borders closed.

My travels to the territory commenced in the early 70s and I have visited hundreds of times, made many good friends and contacts and secured many good orders, all of an honest and straight forward nature. Some of my experiences are detailed in earlier chapters and I did consider moving to live in Doha at one point in my career but felt this would limit my regional activities too much. The Qatari local people are nice, friendly and warm to foreigners and whilst still maintaining strict Muslim rules, are not arrogant in the way of some others, even though they are mega rich. This is a very forward-looking country and, in my opinion, well managed, although some human rights issues and methods of doing business have been questioned, I always felt at home and safe when visiting and completely relaxed.

Now over to Kuwait, which is yet another mega rich territory, thanks to the British finding oil and giving any rights away. This is not a favourite visiting place for me as the Kuwaitis are not, generally speaking, friendly towards or interested in their expat community accepting them as a necessity. Again, strict Muslim rules are adhered to but much good business can be achieved with patience and good local representation. Some of my key friends were Indians, who, in many cases, held senior positions in key local companies, but the decisions are always made by the Kuwaitis in charge.

This small territory, mega rich in oil is not, in my opinion, an ideal place for an expat to live unless working in the local petrochemical industry; believe it or not, I would prefer Saudi Arabia.

The Iraq invasion of Kuwait was horrific with so much damage done, lives lost, people tortured and massive looting of anything and everything moveable. I visited just after the Iraqis had been pushed out but the fired oil fields were causing massive damage and pollution. Live ordnance was everywhere and I actually felt very sorry for the locals, who remained during the war, and for those who managed to flee to the desert.

On into Bahrain, an island of good, friendly people, and a country continuing to maintain a strong relationship with the British. The oil reserves here used to be plentiful, but much has now dried up, so they are not mega rich like some others. The Ruler, Sheikh Essa, is now King and pro-British and a good friend of the UK. Internally, there have been numerous disputes with religious issues at their source as well as human rights matters being questioned, as most have.

I have always enjoyed visiting Bahrain and have done so literally hundreds of times, initially as it was the airline staging hub for many international airlines to refuel en route to the Far East. Later, after the twenty-six-kilometre causeway was built to link Saudi Arabia with Bahrain, it became my preferred route to drive between the two countries, a route also much used by the Saudis as their link into Bahrain as a place for weekend entertainment. In the 70s and 80s, before the emergence of Emirates airline, Gulf Air, owner operated by Bahrain, was the only airline to commute across the Middle East regions. At the time, for locations, timing and frequency, Gulf Air ran an excellent service in every way and crew and pilots were predominantly British.

The USA has its Middle East Navy base in Bahrain and the UK is also building a local Navy base for the region, funded partially by Bahrain. This is presumably a key strategic deployment for both military organisations.

My business interests in Bahrain tended to be smaller than other GCC territories, but nevertheless, it was a strong and straight forward business environment. Life safety was always highly important so fire protection, detection, suppression and management sales were good. Later, with UTC, a major joint venture was set up with the Bahraini Government funding to provide training, however, what a white elephant! Fortunately, I was able to keep this activity at arm's length from my regional responsibility, even though it was linked to their purchase of part of GE fire and security.

Oman has been covered specifically in chapter fifteen, due to my love of the country and its people. However, with regard to its role in the GCC, it is true to say that Oman has often mediated in issues and disputes arising within that Council. My opinion is that this has been helped by the strong link with the UK as well as its own local culture being a key factor.

The United Arab Emirates (UAE) is a major member and influence within the GCC, and is made up of seven Emirates, which are all very individually run by their own ruling families. The UAE was founded on December 2nd, 1971, and was the brain child of the Ruler of Dubai and Ruler of Abu Dhabi. It was initially made up of six Emirates: Abu Dhabi, Dubai, Sharjah, Ajman, Umm Al Quwaim and Fujairah. Ras Al Khaimah joined on February 10th, 1972. Before its foundation, the UAE was made up of Sheikhdoms along the Persian Gulf, and known as The Trucial States, governed by tribal ruling families, which is not so dissimilar to now.

Oil was first discovered in 1958, but is now almost entirely produced by Abu Dhabi, who are mega rich with reported reserves for 150 years. Their petrochemical industry is vast and the majority of oil wells are off-shore.

Dubai oil virtually ran out in the late 70s, so they diversified, very successfully, into tourism, banking, logistics, industry and horse racing.

I started to visit the UAE in the 70s on a regular basis whilst in the defence business and made many influential friends. I have covered much and many of my experiences in previous chapters and only went to live in Dubai in the late 80s. I expected to stay for a couple of years but this turned into twenty!

191

On the surface, Dubai is very liberal and free and easy, which in fact is not the case. It is really a police state, but this has worked well in the rapid expansion of this Emirate and in my opinion, the Ruler and his team have overall done a wonderful job. This job has been made very difficult by the number of expats and differing cultures thrown together in the massive expansion programme. Latterly, and possibly currently, financial support from Abu Dhabi has been of significant importance.

My office base in Dubai, from where we covered markets in Central Europe, Russia, North Africa, the Middle East and parts of Asia, was an excellent location with good air links everywhere.

The expansion in Abu Dhabi has, in my opinion, been much more controlled and perhaps successful. The other Emirates have progressed more slowly and, in many cases, relied on funding from Abu Dubai.

Over the years, I formed a close working relationship with a local company in Abu Dhabi, called Telectron. Very significant sales of fire products were secured within the UAE for Kidde and UTC via this highly professional company run by the Kobty brothers. All the Kobty family became very good friends their true friendship and hospitality are both appreciated and missed.

Overall, my time in the UAE has been excellent and enjoyable, as detailed in previous chapters, but my favourite Emirate is, without doubt, Ras Al Khaimah.

Chapter 17
The USA and Canada

My first crossing of the Atlantic from the UK was in the early 70s to support a British Army equipment cold trial in Canada. The flight was on a Hercules C130, from the RAF Lyneham base to Winnipeg via Gander in Newfoundland. What an experience and actually my first flight in an aeroplane, very noisy and uncomfortable. We sat around the fuselage (of course no in-flight service!) with all the equipment secured in the middle of the aircraft; the toilet had to be seen to be believed. This overseas flight was my first visit to the USA and would include Canada.

As my career progressed, my visits to this vast area became quite varied and extensive and this is an expansion on some of my previously mentioned experiences. The quality of travel naturally improved significantly, initially flying Business Class, later First Class and even on Concorde, all a vast improvement on being RAF cargo.

During my Astra days, I travelled regularly to both the US and Canada as approximately fifty percent of company operations were located across the Atlantic. Our regional office there was based in Washington, near Tysons Corner, and trips there were frequent. However, due to my position, I visited all the business units throughout the country just as often. My move to Fire and Security, latterly as an employee of UTC, a US owned company, brought further operational needs to visit the US and Canada.

The locations of the business units I visited were well spread around the US and near Toronto in Canada. It was interesting that, as a Brit, in every State I travelled through, I was always well received. Although I was interested and pleased to meet people, I cannot say I enjoyed being there and although I was offered a good position to relocate to Washington, I did not consider it positively.

When I joined Kidde, my first job as Regional Director in the Middle East was to do a whistle-stop tour of all the US business units (factories) over a three-week period. This started in early January, which meant thick snow and the whole trip was highly intense. As a new boy in a senior position, but with high level company backing, I was observed with much suspicion and kept at arms-length by some of the business unit senior management; this was understandable but not the easiest way to start a new job whilst meeting everyone and getting to know each operation. Over time, and with knowledge, I became totally accepted and gained the full support and respect of my American brothers but it took a lot of effort, I expect on both sides, to attain that trust, however, achieving increased sales helped us all a lot.

I really liked Boston where I visited often, the seafood was great and the 'natives', friendly. Tennessee was another key experience where everyone was in wonder at my accent, ("I love your accent!" became a refrain) which always helped in the bar! I did so many factory visits to understand the business and build the relationships and co-operation which produced real progress in my business (and theirs). You are only as strong as your people and I won total support for my sales team based in the Middle East, although it was tough going at times.

We had an interesting episode when the Chairman and CEO of Astra Plc and I were flying from Ottawa to Washington after attending an exhibition. Fortunately, I was on a different flight for security and safety reasons, but en route the Chairman was arrested for currency regulation infringements when they stopped him for customs clearance! This was in no way good and ended up with the Chairman spending a day or two in jail; the money was confiscated and deportation followed. Not the most positive situation for a UK PLC and the Chairman of a growing company, but good for a laugh!

Chicago was an interesting destination that I regularly visited as a number of business factories were located there, plus other operational activities in Janesville, Wisconsin, the home of Parker Pens.

One of the Astra factories was in Guelph, in Canada, which is about eighty miles west of Toronto. My visits there were really enjoyable; the town was a bit sleepy but with a Holiday Inn hotel and nice friendly people. On one occasion, I was advised by the hotel reception to drive out to a place called Kitchener for some evening entertainment, which proved to be fantastic. The town was small and initially it seemed like a wasted journey but when buying petrol, the attendant directed me to a certain bar and what a bar it was; 700 yards long and claimed to be the longest in Canada. The building was all at ground level and as big as the famous Hammersmith Palais dance venue in London. The music was live, a large band played to hundreds of people who came from far and wide. What a great place and one I visited on a number of future occasions.

On a very long trip into Houston, Texas, the home of the oil business amongst others, I flew from Dubai with a night stop in the UK, continuing with BA from Gatwick, starting at 1030 hours. Sitting in first class and ready for more than a ten-hour flight, the flight attendant offered me an early drink. I ordered a Johnny Walker Red Label and a little later the steward asked me if everything was okay, I said, "Yes, but my drink wasn't Red Label." He replied that it was Johnny Walker Blue Label, the best, then brought me the bottle to finish off during the long flight, oh happy days.

My visit to Houston was primarily to meet with the procurement organisation dealing with and representing Aramco in Saudi Arabia. To prequalify to provide product to Aramco, a supplier must be approved either in Houston or Leiden in Holland, the latter if the company is European. All a very tortuous process but without formal approval no orders can be achieved from this major customer in the petrochemical business. Many try to beat the system but you cannot, so approvals and formal registration must be obtained and then a locally registered company in Saudi appointed; sounds simple but can take years as I know to my cost.

There I was also talking to Detector Electronics a specialist supplier of high technology detectors, primarily for the oil/petrochemical industry owned by Kidde and subsequently UTC, and a world leader. A well respected and talented company and I enjoyed working with them and had one of their sales engineers on my team based in Dubai.

I visited so many areas of the USA during my career including Los Angeles, Miami, Minneapolis, Philadelphia, New York, Charlotte, Greensboro, Indianapolis, Kansas City, Oklahoma, Fort Sill, Fort Worth, Dallas, Memphis, Atlanta, Raleigh, Newark, Cincinnati and many more. I should have kept a diary; it is difficult to retell stories of each city. In the early days it was all related to defence sales so was limited to military establishments and much of these visits are of a confidential nature which needs to be respected. My days in Fire and Security opened up much more of the US and a little of Canada with the locations of the manufacturing facilities of the group companies of Thorn, Kidde and later the UTC Group.

The Concorde flight I took on 20th April 1989 from London to Washington was definitely the experience of a lifetime, a most exciting flight. I still have the flight certificate signed by Lord King of Wartnaby Chairman and Sir Colin Marshall, CEO of British Airways. Concorde to Washington and returning first class on a BA747 to Heathrow; a ticket price of £3,482 and a flight time outwards of three hours fifteen minutes, then seven and a half hours back to Heathrow!

All friendly, interesting experiences, with many friends made and much business done but still the US as a place to live would not be for me, Canada maybe.

On one occasion I was invited into the home of one of the Astra political advisors for Thanksgiving celebrations, which was enormously kind and quite an experience joining this traditional and large family gathering. There was masses of food and drink for everyone and it was all very convivial and interesting.

It never ceased to amaze me how the eating habits of Americans differed from our own (or should I say, my own?). Fast food seemed to be acceptable even when entertaining guests, particularly at lunchtime, and in abundance. I found this difficult as I was neither much of a lunchtime eater, nor much drawn to fast food outlets. Perhaps this might account for the overweight situation of many, my overweight problem is good food and the bigger the steak the better, or that's my excuse! Another thing I found odd in the US was 'the same only different' element of spoken English, with some very odd words creeping into the general vocabulary.

Chapter 18
Fishing in the Middle East

My significant sea fishing activities started in Oman in the early seventies, whilst involved with the military in Salalah. Usually on a Friday as this was potentially a day off (similar to Sunday in the UK). This entailed driving to a beach called Palm Beach, first following a Bedford truck with a roller on the front to blow up any land mines, then standing in the searing heat and catching very large fish, my biggest achieved there being a ninety-four-pound stingray. Many other varieties were caught; bait was a whole sardine with a metal trace threaded through its body and the hook clipped on. Many years later, a hotel was built on Palm Beach and I visited again, a nostalgic week for a holiday, wonderful memories. I actually drove from Dubai with a night stop in Muscat, about 1600 kilometres. Anyway, back to the early seventies; one Friday I cried off due to a hangover and three of my friends from Airwork Services, based at Hurn in Hampshire, were shot dead by the adu (enemy) whilst fishing on the beach. A very sad day, but many Brits were killed in Salalah in the seventies by the Yemeni terrorists and in accidents, but after all, it was a war zone. I also did a bit of fishing in Muscat at this time which was excellent but so hot

(40 to 50°C) and less coastal breeze, with sometimes ninety percent humidity, making it very uncomfortable.

I first started sea fishing as a young boy, primarily whilst on holiday, always with my dad, and more often than not, off a pier. Southend was a regular venue because Nana and Granddad Pearson lived there at 49 Leamington Road (telephone number 65801); clearly well remembered! Dad and I dug our own bait, primarily rag worm and a few lug worms, which was hard work. We dug for hours after a long walk in boots (the tide goes out a mile at Southend) and sold the whole and unbroken rag worms to the local fishing tackle shop; 100 for a pound! The broken worms we took for our own fishing off the pier. We only caught small fish and usually flat fish like plaice, dabs, dover sole, plus whiting and a few others but all good fun. Basically, if there was a river, a lake or sea, I had to go fishing. I must have been a real pain in the backside as a child!

When in Saudi Arabia, I did more fishing, but without the same success, even though the Red Sea was wonderful, but I did not try too hard there as being on the beach was not safe. The move to Dubai was a welcome change for so many reasons and fishing was certainly one of them.

In the early days in Dubai, before I lived there, I suggested to a British military officer and friend that we should take his son fishing on the Creek at the side of a road bridge. He went and bought some tackle and a rod with my advice and with some bait (mackerel and prawns), we went to try our luck. Against my advice, he left his rod a few feet away whilst in deep water, and waiting for a bite. It must be assumed it was Moby Dick, or something very similar, because it took the bait, rod and line. So much for my teaching, but at least it proved some very large fish were in the Creek and laughing at us. This military officer, now retired, became a long-term friend to this day and I have no doubt that when his son reads this, he will remember his first fishing trip and laugh.

The prime bait in Dubai was mackerel and my method was to remove the head and tail, then, with the sides filleted and cut into big pieces, plus a big hook, wire trace and a sliding lead weight, it proved very successful. The line was 35 lbs, breaking strain with 300 yards on the reel and this worked well. The rod was not a beach caster as such, but about twelve-feet so I could cast out about eighty yards. My rest was a piece of pipe with a welded spike to mount vertically in the sand. Once in the water, I stood within arms-length of the rod, otherwise, when a fish took the bait, the rod would be lost if I could not hang on immediately. It often took twenty minutes to land the fish and sometimes it was so big I had to cut the line and let it go so plenty of stories of 'the one that got away'. All excellent fun and I caught many fish with very few blank days but plenty of sun burn!

Fishing in Dubai with Chris Rutt and friends was so pleasurable and competitive that I find it difficult to describe just how good it was. We usually fished for a few dirhams wager for added challenge and ended up in the pub in the evening, often the Ramada, having driven about hundred miles each way to our favourite fishing place, although we did explore widely and found some excellent fishing places. We caught many different species big and small, some we took home to eat, most were thrown back. Fishing days were mainly Fridays, sometimes Saturday as well, morning to late afternoon. Chris was a great guy and I am sorry we have lost touch over time. The time spent with him and my friends was truly special. Our favourite and best venue was at Rams, in the north of the UAE, which, apart from the long drive, entailed a walk across the rocks out to sea for about a mile. Highly dodgy whilst carrying all the fishing gear and picnic, then the catch on the way back, it was also extremely hot with temperatures well over 40 C most of the time. Very happy days.

Fujairah, an eastern Emirate of the UAE is a rocky mountainous area with an ongoing quarrying industry. Much of the lowland oases were transformed for large scale agriculture which has been big and successful investment providing UAE local produce – though most is imported from surrounding countries. The Friday Market, running a few kilometres down each side of the highway on the route to Fujairah, provided an interesting stop selling just about everything. The Asian carpet vendors there were the best and a good place to take business and personal visitors, I brought them a lot of business!

The Fujairah coastline being a shipping channel with refuelling and dry dock services; there could always be seen along the horizon an interesting, varied line-up of ships. With Thorn Security, Kidde and UTC, we did a fair amount of fire protection and security business in the Emirate. The city itself is large, with local hotels, residence blocks and all the services, medical, commercial and civil. Latterly, several coastal, tourist hotels were built with their private sandy beaches and permitted swimming to enjoy. The old original Hilton however remained a favourite of mine and it seemed likewise to long-standing expat residents of Fujairah and also much used by military on furlough.

Further up that coast, towards Khor Fakkan, exploring, I found some great fishing spots, on one occasion pulling in a huge sand shark, which was difficult to handle more so as it was sundown and night always felt like a blanket interest had made me stay too long – watching the turtles swimming by was quite a distraction! Anyway, managed to get the shark onto its back, the hook out and see it off safely back into the sea before packing up and picking my way back to the car.

We explored many places all over the UAE in all the Emirates but without doubt, Rams was the cream and produced some wonderful fish. I never ventured into boat fishing which seemed too easy; I always fished off the beach and where possible have the car not too far away due to the heat. Fishing in Dubai itself was basically a waste of time due to all the dredging and building works which ruined the fishing, unless you travelled miles off shore. The Creek in the town was not bad for a quick hour or two but I usually only caught catfish but many other species were there, I just found it hard to catch them.

I bought two spare rods, reels and tackle to enable friends and business colleagues to come out with me. A picnic on the beach or barbeque was normal, but drinking alcohol in public being illegal; some tactics took place. Many friends, some of whom had never fished before had very good days out and caught sizeable fish.

When Mum and Dad came to stay and members of the family, including Annette in the early days, many different fish were caught. On one occasion, on a visit when Dad was in his 80s, he was sitting on a folding chair on the sand, fishing rod in hand and yelled out for help with a large fish hooked which was about to pull him in. I landed it and it was a stingray well over twenty-five pounds; they always go to ground for a while when first hooked, it can be a long match!

Sea fishing is not really for me, I am a freshwater coarse fisherman at heart but in the Gulf, you only have sea (no rivers) and I did not fish in other Middle Eastern countries where there are rivers, for example, Iraq. My good friend, Sid Wright, visited a number of times and we enjoyed fishing together and he caught some nice fish (think they must have been retards).

The best eating fish in the Arab world is often considered to be fresh water fish if available. Iraq is a very good example, where, along the banks of the Tigris River live barbel, they are kept in old baths which you choose from, they kill it in front of you and take it to the restaurant to be smoked. The dish is called Masgouf and you sit in the open on the river bank to eat with rats as big as cats at your feet!

During my many visits to Muscat by road from Dubai, I stopped off at lots of places to do a bit of fishing. These places were frequently quite remote and seldom visited by expats which made it even more interesting. Some extraordinary shells and beach flotsam made these stops great for beachcombing and my shell collection became vast. Driving up the west coast of the UAE, through Ras Al Khaimah and Rams onwards to the Omani border at Shams then into the north of Oman was also a fantastic experience, normally staying at the Golden Tulip Hotel or one or two others at Khasab. This was always a delight.

It is true to say that fishing in the Middle East over all those years and discovering lots of new places was always a joy and I have some wonderful memories which were seriously enhanced by some of my fishing partners. Many fish were caught; rays, catfish, parrot fish, trigger fish, yellow jack, barracuda, snapper, sole and such a lot of others. Much to the Arabs' amazement, most were thrown back alive; I only kept fish to eat occasionally.

Chapter 19
Political Matters

The political issues primarily related to my experiences in business are all linked to the darker side of the defence industry. This is high value business, whether for UK MOD, or for export and therefore, the potential profits are big. Most UK defence manufacturers have formal arrangements with politicians on their boards as non-executive directors, plus more covert arrangements with others. The security services also play a major part, whether it be MI5 or MI6, and this is obviously of a covert nature. I met with security personnel on a regular basis at various locations, but an apartment in Dolphin Square was often used as a good venue in London and very secure. This apartment block used by many famous people as a residence or for clandestine meetings, could tell many stories if the walls could speak!

The rules for the export of defence related products from the UK are very clearly defined and export licences need to be in place before goods are shipped. Authority also needs to be obtained before a defence product is formally promoted in a territory, a precursor to obtaining an export licence.

Now we come to the first grey area. If, for example, country X asked a British company to quote for let us say some 130 mm shells that they manufacture in-house and an export licence has been obtained. Is country X the real end user or is the product being shipped on to a third party? If the latter is the case and the goods are shipped from the UK, it is illegal; the company would be in serious trouble and employees jailed. A good sales manager or sales director should know or have a very good idea if an enquiry is genuine but the wish to gain a lucrative order might cloud the judgement a little, a very dangerous game to play. Another grey area is the manipulation of the issue of granting an export licence approval and this is where 'political' influence may become useful, formally or covertly, whichever way it can be a very lucrative activity for those involved. In-country agents or facilitators can also cause major issues but can also provide very useful local support, however, some may use part of their 'commission' to grease the wheels, which can create further major issues. The levels of commission paid can also be an indicator if something is dodgy so an experienced salesman is always on the lookout for inappropriate activities which could compromise his company or himself.

Back to politicians, who love the intrigue and dealings related to defence business, and this, to my knowledge, is a very significant number; some may also be linked to the security services, or think they are! Whilst the lobby rules in Parliament are strict, the opportunity does exist for those rules to be bent and abused and, I believe, this does happen in order to assist the large defence conglomerates as well as smaller defence companies.

In my experience, most politicians do stick to the rules and formally declare their business interests through the established channels. They are also, more often than not, formally appointed as non-executive directors of a particular company, which is not always defence-oriented. The level of annual remuneration for non-executive directors can often be quite modest, depending on the MP's status, but an annual performance bonus can be a major revenue boost. Shareholdings or pension options are also areas of flexibility and without doubt, expense claims on the company, another area of potential gain. My involvement with MPs was normally limited to London parties and defence exhibitions where many influential politicians would attend. Overseas exhibitions are always popular as the trips are normally all expenses paid and in defence significant orders maybe up for grabs. Whilst at the Richard Unwin Group, we had two MPs as non-executive directors who were honest, had a high degree of integrity in every respect and did provide good positive advice in a straightforward manner, which helped me a lot when MD. At Astra Holdings PLC, we had the benefit of the appointment of the perhaps notorious Jonathan Aitkin as a non-executive director of Astra Defence Systems. He was high profile, as a minister at the Treasury, with a fantastic pedigree and I liked him and initially respected his advice and guidance. We sat on the same board of Astra Defence Systems and met at various functions on many occasions. My view was that in the defence environment, his wealth of experience and contacts in many parts of the world, particularly the Middle East, was invaluable and he was an asset in defence activities, particularly for export. However, things started to go wrong when issues in a number of areas were raised in the media and press, which resulted in Jonathan resigning as an MP and, after many legal and court appearances, going to jail. My opinion is that he went too far, thought he could walk on water and committed the fundamental sin to lie to the House and the media – again, my opinion, but a great loss to UK Limited. During this time, many well-known and high-profile political figures were involved with defence projects either directly or indirectly particularly related to Iraq and Saudi Arabia but it would be inappropriate for me to name them.

Senior serving military officers also become deeply involved with defence sales, but I believe they see this as part of their duty and do not seek payback; just a way to support UK export activities. Some of these officers often take up employment with defence companies on their retirement from the services.

During my career in the defence business, exporting was my primary activity, so export permission was something I lived with on a daily basis. Politicians became more and more important and rubbing shoulders with them at London parties or events was perhaps the best way to establish initial contacts. I attended so many events and made some friends and many contacts on the political scene. The well-known 'arms dealers', who I met regularly in the course of business, were also a major route to market and they were often offering 'incentives'. To agree to this is the kiss of death and I am so glad that I never accepted this route other than perhaps a lunch or dinner and drinks for genuine business discussions and was well-known in the business as 'the straight guy'.

I could name many high-level personalities that I had contact with, which would run into a very large number, plus in-depth details of what went on, but this would be inappropriate; my lips remain sealed and nothing will change this stance. A number of approaches have been made to me by the media over the years (newspapers and television) for my story, particularly related to Astra Plc with large sums of money offered, but my response has been, and still is, 'no comment'. As the Group Sales and Marketing Director of Astra, I certainly knew answers to many of the questions, and perhaps, held some pieces of the jigsaw, but I never gave evidence at any of the enquiries like the Scott enquiry and various Select Committees; I wonder why! One serious attempt on my life was enough and the final straw and the main reason I left the job I loved in defence; I resigned and moved into commercial business but still primarily for export and there I stayed.

The 'accident' happened on the M4, near the Bristol turn off, and occurred at 0730 hours, whilst I was driving south. I was in my 4Ltr Jaguar XJ6, and alone in the fast lane doing about 70 or perhaps a little more. Suddenly a fuel tanker pulled into the fast lane at 90° to the traffic and a large Mercedes van blocked my near side so I had nowhere to go. I hit the tanker over its wheel, arches at full speed, with no time to brake. The impact was enormous and I should have died; the engine was under the car but I managed to get out of the driver's side window. The fuel tanker had ruptured so was gushing fuel everywhere but fortunately it was diesel and did not ignite. When the police arrived within minutes and asked, "Where is the body from the Jaguar?"

I said, "That's me." To cut the story short, I was in the hospital for a week or so, with various serious injuries, but lived to tell the tale and the car, only a few weeks old, was a total write-off. The M4 was closed in both directions for approximately four hours and the drivers of the other two vehicles, though injured, had disappeared. Investigation proved the vehicles had been hired on false credit cards but the drivers were never traced! The police said they believed that it was attempted murder; could it have been the Israelis or Iraqis, we will never know!

Overall, defence can be a very dirty business if you are naive, stupid or just greedy, but very interesting and always challenging. I look back fondly on a job I believe was well done and a most enjoyable and interesting part of my life; none of which I regret.

The Jaguar After The Crash I Walked Away From!

Chapter 20
Consultancy

After my bomb shell resignation from UTC, I expected to be told to leave immediately, which would be normal company procedure; however, in my case not so. I was made to work my full notice period and instructed not to advise anyone that I was leaving; this was a direct order and made my life very difficult. I was high profile in the region and wanted to advise my many friends and contacts, but this was not initially possible, even to my direct staff but, typical of UTC senior management. After a month or so, I decided to ignore the instruction and advised my staff in confidence and started to advise key contacts throughout the region.

I was asked to interview a potential successor but about an hour before the interview, an insider and friend advised me that he had already been appointed and the interview was a sham! I went ahead and recommended his appointment and never let on that I knew about the con. My successor would not have been my choice but he was a very reasonable guy and subsequently treated me with respect and understanding, but I believe was instrumental in destroying the Middle East operation that I had established; perhaps this was inevitable progress under UTC rule!

I was offered a one-year consultancy and negotiated the long and complex agreement, which took many weeks. The final draft employed me for twelve days a month for one year, with all the current perks of MD and similar salary and they reluctantly agreed to continue with business class travel; not a bad deal and still living in Dubai, tax free. I accepted the offer, signed on the bottom line and effectively reported to my successor. Then a problem; how would UTC pay me, which I thought was no problem, just continue as I was originally paid. This was unacceptable to UTC as paying a consultant could be seen as an issue in law and be unethical. I therefore had to set up my own consultancy company in the UAE, which could then issue a formal invoice for consultancy services and any expenses on a monthly basis. UTC agreed to meet the set-up costs and running costs.

I decided to form my consultancy company in the Ras Al Khaimah (RAK) Free Zone, which is based about a hundred miles to the north of Dubai. This Free Zone offers Middle East operating companies with working or token offices and production manufacturing companies plus logistic companies acting as a distribution hub. It was much friendlier, lower cost and more flexible than the famous Jebel Ali Free Zone in Dubai. It is a long process to form a company, whatever they say, and the banking element is the most difficult, but once done, everything runs smoothly; no VAT and no tax. I named my company Hammond Consult FZE after my dad's middle name, 'Hammond', which was also one of his uncle's names. This company did not trade as such and had no trading licence; it was only licensed as a representative consultancy office. My logo was a fisherman, with a rod and line, standing fishing in blue, a close friend's idea which I adopted and loved. When asked what the logo represented, and what did it mean, my answer was, "I am angling for business." Ho, ho. I can say that I am very experienced at setting up operations in a UAE Free Zone, which I wish I could use to help others who could well benefit from a Free Zone status in the region.

My consultancy started and it was quite strange, having been supremo for so long and now having no power and side-lined. However, I must say that my successor did treat me with respect and in a kindly manner. He had strong ideas to bring all the business units into his way of thinking, which I did not agree with, but offered to do a tour and provide presentations to support his strategy, his response was to say, "No thanks, f… them." In my opinion, the first big mistake.

I continued to travel a lot to specific territories, including Kuwait, Saudi Arabia, Qatar and many others where there were specific issues that had to be addressed; you could say that I became a 'Mr Fix-it'. I also had some spare time, a first for a long time, so fishing and golf started to be quite important. The established JVs were all on the way to being cancelled, with the exception of the UAE with Zener and the agreement with Abdulla was getting worse by the day. The UTC overall strategy for the region was breaking down what I had built up and for me it was very sad.

My second consultancy year required a new agreement, which proved to be a real epic, primarily due to the business class travel element, as I was the only employee who enjoyed this luxury. We finally agreed a compromise of wording and I still flew business class most of the time. The Middle East operation was now falling apart, with massive cost increases with plush new offices, lots more staff and major reductions in order intake, so the cost of sales went through the roof.

Further strategic changes were being actioned with the joining of other UTC companies, so my days were numbered, and I was very glad to conclude my second consultancy year. I can safely say that UTC had made my fifteen years of excellent business for Kidde a wasted effort! I am not bitter, just very disappointed.

I met up with an old friend of many years in Dubai, who was now the MD of Luxfer, the leading manufacturer of aluminium gas cylinders; he was now based in the UK. He had issues with manufacturing activities in India and current sales in the Middle East and thought I might be interested in providing some consultancy effort using my extensive contacts list. This short-term activity proved very interesting with a number of visits to India and the Middle East region working with their formal distributors who were based in Dubai. This really was an interesting few months and I was treated very well by Luxfer personnel and their agents and I hope that my experience proved to be a benefit.

During this time I was in discussion with an old adversary Nitin Shah who was the MD of the Nitin Fire Group in India, FSL in the UK and NewAge in Dubai. Over the years I had blocked all efforts by Nitin to work with Kidde and UTC as a distributor for various reasons, one of which was unethical practices or rumours of such. However, Nitin approached me to work as a consultant for his group, working out of the NewAge offices in Dubai primarily to promote export sales attend exhibitions and give presentations to potential investors.

The plan was flexible, with an average of ten working days a month, at a daily rate plus expenses. I accepted the offer and spent, about the next three years, helping Nitin with various projects and activities which entailed commuting from the UK to Dubai every month. I guess what he wanted was a well-known face from the fire industry to be part of his senior team to improve his credibility. I have to say, I learned to like Nitin, and he always treated me well, with respect and introduced me to people as "The man who knows everyone." The time working with Nitin was made easier due to his key advisor and PA, Vilsy. She ran the office in all respects and seemed to have his complete trust, although, in my opinion, should have been the office manager. Totally trustworthy, very professional and confidential and was the rock of the Dubai operation. She used her power to good effect at all times and really helped me. The Dubai Office also had some other good support staff but they were all in fear of Nitin and the office was certainly run on fear; the only exception being Vilsy and perhaps myself. This fear factor is perhaps the norm in the Indian culture, which I consider to be a significant weakness.

I enjoyed my time within his group but turned down various full-time roles which he offered on a regular basis. It was disappointing when our business relationship came to an end due to financial issues within the group. We remain friends and if asked for help or advice, I would be pleased to step in.

I am still being approached to provide consultancy services by one or two key contacts, primarily in the Middle East, but to date have declined.

Chapter 21
Retirement, the Twilight Years

Like many, I am finding adapting to retirement to be a difficult time. I guess I was a workaholic for most of my working life and I continue to miss the challenges it brought, so it is hard to accept a quiet life; in fact, it is more than just boring. Fishing and golf are fine but what to do with the rest of the week? I also miss meeting so many of my overseas friends, particularly in Qatar and the UAE. That part of my working life was so important to me, meeting people, I think it helped my overall success as, for some reason, I got on with people and they trusted me.

Without doubt, a key factor is health, we cannot arrange the roll of the health dice; it is in the lap of the gods, but we can try to help a little towards living to a ripe old age. On my plus side, all my family have lived long (middle 90s) but they were a different generation, who had good diets due to custom and finance and the unimaginable hardship of war. I have spent my life working too hard, eating too much and the wrong things, plus drinking far too much alcohol; late nights, etcetera, but fortunately never smoking. So, what to do? Eat a bit less, drink a lot less and get more exercise, but overall, keep happy; I do hope this helps!

Having made the retirement decision and concluded about five years doing consultancy, the health situation started to raise its ugly head! First came a bout of kidney pain, which I recognised well, having passed more than a hundred stones over the years, but this was a bit different. The consultant advised me that I had two stones that were over a centimetre and surgery was the only answer, so off to private hospital, home after a few days and all seemed well, but then a relapse with sepsis; oh joy. Into an NHS hospital this time and I believe it may have been touch and go for a while, but after about two and half weeks, was back home to fully recover. Not a nice experience but as I have always said, you cannot keep a good man down. However, the downside was that the surgeon left a bit of stone behind, he said, "Sorry but it is only small."

Some four years later, it has grown to at least nine-mm, so more surgery will be needed sooner or later because it is too big to pass!

Another issue arose with a similar problem to one I had had in Dubai some years earlier, which required a hospital procedure at that time. This time, however, it was much worse; ambulance to A&E with serious internal bleeding which proved to be two ulcers; after surgery and blood transfusions and another two and a half weeks in hospital, back home again to fully recover.

Later came further surgery for shoulder and knee problems but nothing else of a serious nature so far, thank goodness, but I suppose, as I am now seventy-six and have exceeded my three score and ten, everything is now a bonus. Being retired seems to bring on illness or is it just old age, not working or payback time for being so healthy for ninety-nine percent of my life?

I started collecting Goss China more than fifty years ago and initially selected cottages; these being quite rare. They were generally replicas of famous people's birth places and my idea was to buy three or four and sell them on at a profit, but then I decided I liked them and started collecting. I now have all those known to have been made with many of the variations and the collection totals well over 200 pieces, kept safely at a bank. I also expanded to collect Goss Parian ware busts and again have a large collection of more than a hundred pieces. William Henry Goss was born in 1833 and produced his trademark pottery in the first period 1858 to 1887 in his factory in Stoke-on-Trent. The second period, which was 1881 to 1934, was perhaps the most prolific for William Henry and the third period, dated 1929 to 1939, included items manufactured in a number of factories and by some others, but usually marked W H Goss in various forms. Heraldic China models are the most well-known, but cottages and Parian busts are the most sought after and can be very rare and valuable. My thanks for encouraging my collecting must go to Nicholas and Lynda Pine, the world authority on W H Goss, and who supplied many of my rarest pieces.

I do keep in touch with a number of my business friends and colleagues who are still alive and kicking, which quite often involves a lot of talking about the old days and work experiences but it does pass some of the time pleasantly. My collection of W H Goss China gives me much pleasure, particularly as it's one of the best known to exist and meeting up with other serious collectors is always a good event that I enjoy.

In December 2019 I had an invitation for a Christmas lunch by a contact from Baku, Azerbaijan, who I had not seen for about twenty years; what a surprise. It was a very kind invitation and they gave me wonderful hospitality at The Oxford Golf Club and Spa; I am so glad I accepted and met everyone again and I sincerely hope we meet again in the future.

I have maintained my contact and good friendship with Richard Unwin, who invited me to join the board of a company he was forming in the UK to provide export advice to UK companies wishing to expand into new markets after Brexit; I accepted. However, after some months of enjoyable work, I decided, for a number of personal reasons, to step down and resign. Not what I wanted to do but circumstances made the decision for me; I really had no choice.

It is, in many ways, nice to be able to see my family (the tribe!) after spending so much time travelling away from home and living in Dubai for approximately twenty years, but they have their own lives to live; perhaps this book will be of interest to them! My very, very good friend, Sid Wright, is still my oldest friend and I try to see him whenever I can. I cannot say what his continued friendship and meetings mean to me, he is one of the best.

I have not been a holiday person for many years and this pastime does not appeal and I am very happy not to board an aircraft ever again, however, I could be persuaded to visit the sun as I do miss the warmth. I doubt I will travel to Dubai again, but Oman could be a possibility, or maybe Europe; the latter preferably by car. I would like to make a visit to some of the war graves in France and, having visited the cemetery in Thailand at the Bridge over the river Kwai, I know how emotional this can be but very rewarding and humbling.

My travels have taken me all over the world, visiting more than a hundred countries, but have only actually lived in England and the UAE. I have to admit that while I have experienced so much from global travel, I can remember feeling a little ashamed that many of my foreign visitors, that I took sightseeing in London over the years, knew more of our history than I! Perhaps this is the time to explore a lot more of the motherland – when the weather is good!

Being retired is a challenge in itself but I have so much to be thankful for and a lot of different memories to look back on, happy days.

Chapter 22
The Next Challenge

In retirement, my main problem has been what to do with my own time now, how to keep my brain working? I may have actually been giving up the fight through the stupid thought that I was too old and finished. Then my very good friend, Larry, said to me, "You must write the book and why not some lecturing about exporting and forming Joint Ventures; a university could be very interested." This pricked my ears up and certainly, writing this autobiography has brought back some new life into this old dog, taxing brain and memory. Perhaps, as he suggested; my wealth of experience and global knowledge of business could be very interesting, useful and beneficial to young budding executives, maybe I should give it a go! At the moment it is a thought but I am interested to find out more!

The Brexit issue, which I followed closely, has gone on for years and been a debacle but now completed, we as a country, need to attack the next, even more important, phase, like trade deals, etcetera. In my opinion, we should form Free Zones in many places to enable goods to be imported free of duty, worked on and re-exported free of duty! This system works so well in the UAE and I know it backwards; perhaps I should be offering my services to our government or interested companies.

So, what is next? Another, but more interesting, book, of fiction this time; could this be my new vocation? Many interesting titles come to mind like 'The Defence Industry in the UK' but that would be non-fiction! It would have to include my excellent support writer, or it's just not going to happen. I had thought a first draft would take about six months but all being well, it has been done within a month; the second draft may take a similar time. I do hope there's an interested publisher out there!

Writing this has made me realise just how lucky I have been and how much I owe to so many people, many of whom it is too late to thank personally as they have passed on. I do sometimes think of Mum, when I was a youngster, saying, "You will never make anything of yourself, stick to fishing." She would be very surprised now and my reading has improved, so has my typing, thanks to this book.

God bless you all for reading this story of my progression through life, which has been an eventful and great adventure and with much more to come, I hope.

Hammond Consult FZE

Dad on his 90th Birthday   Small self at 3 years old

Appendix

A time line of my progress through life:

1945 I arrived, Born E17

1950 Greenford Infants school

1952 Costains junior school

1956 Horsenden Secondary School

1961 Passed three "O" levels

1961 Started EMI Apprenticeship

1966 Completed Apprenticeship

1966 Married Annette Holland

1966 Passed ONC

1967 Joined PDS team

1968 Passed HNC

1969 Maria born

1969 Joined Cymbeline Project

1969 Based Larkhill Artillery for four years

1973 Claire born

1976 Tina born

1981 Joined Central Marketing

1983 Left EMI Electronics

1983 Joined Richard Unwin International

1986 Transferred to Astra Holdings

1987 Appointed Group Sales and Marketing Director

1988 Appointed Director Astra Defence Systems

1990 Resigned Astra Holdings PLC

1990 Joined Hall and Watts Middle East

1992 Left Hall & Watts (redundant)

1992 Re-joined EMI

1992 Appointed Resident Manager EMI in Kingdom of Saudi Arabia

1993 Joined Thorn EMI Security: Management Buy-Out

1995 Left Thorn EMI (redundant)

1995 Joined Kidde, Regional Director Middle East, Dubai

2006 UTC takeover. Managing Director, Middle East, Russia, Central Europe and the CIS

2012 Took early Retirement

2012 Formed Consultancy Company

Hammond Consult FZE, Ras Al Khaimah, UAE